Meet FULTON SHEEN

· Beloved Preacher and Teacher of the Word ·

JANEL RODRIGUEZ

SERVANT BOOKS

PUBLISHED BY ST. ANTHONY MESSENGER PRESS
CINCINNATI, OHIO

Excerpts from *Peace of Soul* by Fulton Sheen, copyright © 1996. Used with permission of Liguori Publications, Liguori, MO 63057. 1-800-325-9521.

Excerpts from *Lift Up Your Heart* by Fulton Sheen, copyright © 1997. Used with permission of Liguori Publications, Liguori, MO 63057. 1-800-325-9521.

Unless otherwise noted, Scripture passages have been taken from the *Revised Standard Version*, Catholic edition. Copyright 1946, 1952, 1971 by the Division of Christian Education of the National Council of Churches of Christ in the USA. Used by permission. All rights reserved.

Cover and book design by Mark Sullivan
Cover photo © Bettmann/CORBIS

LIBRARY OF CONGRESS CATALOGING-IN-PUBLICATION DATA
Rodriguez, Janel.
 Meet Fulton Sheen : beloved teacher and preacher of the Word / Janel
Rodriguez.
    p. cm.
 Includes bibliographical references.
 ISBN-13: 978-0-86716-709-2 (pbk. : alk. paper)
 ISBN-10: 0-86716-709-2 (pbk. : alk. paper) 1. Sheen, Fulton J. (Fulton
John), 1895-1979. 2. Catholic Church—United States—Bishops—Biography. I.
Title.

BX4705.S612R63 2006
282.092—dc22

                                                          2006003756

ISBN-13: 978-0-86716-709-2
ISBN-10: 0-86716-709-2

Published by Servant Books, an imprint of
St. Anthony Messenger Press.
28 W. Liberty St.
Cincinnati, OH 45202
www.AmericanCatholic.org

Printed in the United States of America.

Printed on acid-free paper.

06 07 08 09 10 5 4 3 2 1

This book is dedicated to all the priests who, as servants of God,
have inspired and strengthened my faith by their example, especially
Father Jack Canning, O. CARM.,
a priest in love with prayer and the Eucharist.

And to the friars and third order members in the
Carmelite Order of North America
in the Provinces of St. Elias and The Most Pure Heart of Mary.

Flos Carmeli

Contents

. . . . .

Acknowledgments

I WISH TO EXTEND A SPECIAL THANK YOU TO EACH OF the following people:

First and foremost, I am grateful to Mike Aquilina for his enthusiastic support and guidance. He is truly a man of God and a gentle, giving soul. Without his involvement in my career, I would not have been able to write this book.

I also would like to thank my editor, Cynthia Cavnar, who saw this book through from start to finish and whose wisdom and experience have been of invaluable help to me. Christian publishing is richer for her professional presence and grace.

My parents, Deacon Arnaldo Rodriguez and Gladys Rodriguez, are tremendously responsible for the person I am today. Their years of parental love, strong faith and encouragement are ever-present gifts in my life for which I will never be able to properly thank them.

James and Anne Berrettini, please accept my gratitude for your good words and for your friendship. To Carmelite Father Linus Ryan and Greg Hildebrandt, I also wish to express thanks: the information you both provided helped me make this book fresher and more informative.

Last but not least I thank my sister, Jennifer Rodriguez, who patiently withstood my hours of hogging the computer and thoughtfully looked the other way as I constructed sloppy towers of paper, books and other research material all over our new home. I feel most blessed to know I can always rely on her understanding. (Thanks, Twin!)

May the Lord continue to bless each one of you.

Janel Rodriguez
November 2005

Foreword

WHETHER YOU ARE IN THE ABOVE-FIFTY-FIVE-YEAR-OLD crowd for whom "Bishop Fulton J. Sheen" was a common household name while growing up, or if you only came to know of him by hearsay in more recent years, you are going to love reading *Meet Fulton Sheen: Beloved Preacher and Teacher of the Word*.

In a very readable and attractive style, author Janel Rodriguez presents the main stages of Archbishop Sheen's life and work while interweaving many personal incidents that bring out the true character of this great churchman. I was even pleasantly surprised to find the story of my own ordination by then Bishop (later Archbishop) Sheen and all that surrounded it as part of Janel's biography. She clearly presents the life of Archbishop Sheen as it truly was: a rare but extraordinary blending of natural gifts and supernatural graces. Endowed with a keen intellect, Archbishop Sheen used it to become a gifted teacher, prolific writer and effective preacher.

Furthermore, Archbishop Sheen was the first, and I believe still greatest, media voice of the Catholic church in America. For over thirty years, through both radio and television, his "electronic evangelization" inspired millions of people, both Catholics and non-Catholics alike, with the message that all human life has a God-given purpose and is always worth living.

Despite great achievements and immense popularity, Archbishop Sheen was no stranger to the taste of failure and especially rejection. But through it all, his ardent love of Jesus Christ and our Blessed Lady and his loyalty to the church and her mission generated the enormous zeal that motivated him constantly. It is no wonder that the competent ecclesiastical authorities have declared him a "Servant of God" whose life is worthy of investigation as a possible saint in the Catholic church.

No one summed up his life better than our late Holy Father John Paul II when he embraced Archbishop Sheen in the sanctuary of St. Patrick Cathedral in New York City and said to him: "You have written and spoken well of the Lord Jesus. You are a loyal son of the Church."

Once you start reading this book, I am sure that you will find it difficult to put it down!

Fr. Andrew Apostoli, C.F.R.
Vice-postulator for the Cause of the Servant of God
Archbishop Fulton J. Sheen

❦ I ❦

A Prophecy for a Prophet

BISHOP FULTON J. SHEEN WOULD LATER COMPARE THE crashing sound to the "intensity of decibels"[1] in an atomic explosion. He was eight years old and serving as an altar boy in Peoria, Illinois. As he was handling the wine cruet, young Fulton suddenly felt it slip from his hand to meet the marble floor.

There could not have been a worse combination of factors: glass hitting marble in a cavernous building, in the middle of the most important religious rite in the Catholic church, not in just any church but in St. Mary Cathedral and not in the presence of just any priest but before Bishop John L. Spalding himself. Needless to say, Fulton was "frightened to death."[2]

Bishop Spalding waited until the end of Mass to speak with the boy who had made such a spectacle of himself.

Taking the frightened Fulton aside, the bishop asked something surprising. He wanted to know what school Fulton planned to attend when he was older.

Fulton replied, "Spalding Institute." It was unintentional flattery. The local Catholic high school was named after the bishop.

Bishop Spalding shook his head. His question referred to higher education than that. He asked if Fulton had ever heard of a university called Louvain. The boy had not.

The bishop then instructed him, "You go home and tell your mother that I said when you get big you are to go to Louvain, and someday you will be just as I am."

Later that day Fulton relayed to his mother what the bishop had said. She told her son that Louvain was located in Belgium and was one of the "greatest universities in the world."[3]

Neither mother nor son would think more of the incident for some time. They didn't know that while Bishop Spalding was well-respected as a learned man of God and prolific writer of essays, he was apparently endowed with the gift of prophecy as well. When Fulton Sheen "got big," he did attend Louvain. Later he would distinguish himself for his intellectual gifts and his way with words, much as Bishop Spalding had done. He would go on to become a respected priest and finally, just like Spalding, a successor to the apostles: a bishop in the Roman Catholic church.

Fulton J. Sheen would also "get big" in ways not foretold by Bishop Spalding. He would grow to a fame and influence of a scope larger than that of any other American bishop before him or after, educating millions on the teachings of the church and converting a great number of souls to Christ.

HUMBLE BEGINNINGS

The ability to identify a young man's vocation to the priesthood seems to have been Sheen's also, and it began when he recognized his own call. While many priests have suffered through discernment periods, it appears Sheen never endured that particular struggle. The bishop wrote in his autobiography that he could not remember a time in his life when he did not want to become a priest.[4] In fact, while "watching young corn come up under [his] eyes" when he was growing up on a farm in Illinois, he would "say the rosary begging for a vocation."[5]

Although this was the serious truth, he said it with a twinkle in his eye, for young Fulton intensely disliked farm life. This is not surprising, as it is difficult to reconcile the famous image of an erudite and citified bishop with that of a rugged, earthy child who plowed fields and milked cows. A neighbor of the Sheens in Peoria, Billy Ryan, noted Fulton's lack of farming skills and decided that the boy would grow up to be rather useless (the exact quote was that he would never be "worth a damn"). Ryan complained that Fulton always had "his nose in a book."[6]

Fulton was not completely useless, however. An extra pair of hands on a farm is always helpful, and help Fulton did. After all, it wasn't the hard work Fulton despised. On the contrary, a strong work ethic was a value his parents pressed upon him from an early age and one he took to heart. He learned it well through his chores and responsibilities on the

farm, and it was a virtue that would prove enormously ben-
eficial throughout his life.

Fulton simply had no aptitude for farm work, seeing it
as a lot of expended energy in order to get nowhere.
Meanwhile, there was another area in his life for which
Fulton showed great natural aptitude and to which he dili-
gently applied himself: school. Fulton was a scholastic star
and would go on to earn many academic achievements.

That young Fulton and his brothers, Joseph, Thomas
and Aloysius, receive a proper education was a goal of primary importance to their parents. Morris Newton Sheen
(or "Newt") and his wife Delia were of humble means, but
they made sure to enroll all of their children in Catholic
schools. Each of their sons went on to a successful career:
Joe in law, Tom in medicine, Al in industry and Fulton, of
course, in the church.

A HOLY MOTHER

Fulton J. Sheen was born Peter Fulton Sheen on May 8,
1895, in El Paso, Illinois. The oldest of four boys, he was
named Peter after his father's father, and Fulton was his
mother's maiden name. Delia's parents, John and Mary
Fulton, often looked after Peter. The story goes that they
were with the boy so much that he was referred to as "the
Fultons' boy," which was later shortened to "Fulton." In his
autobiography Sheen wrote that when his grandparents
enrolled him in parochial school and were asked the name
of their grandson, John Fulton replied simply, "It's Fulton."[7]

Fulton's mother was a particularly devout Catholic.
The word most often used to describe her was *saintly*.[8] In

fact, it was her piety that formed her husband's faith: Newt joined the church in order to marry her. It was not long before he was as committed to the faith as she was.

There is no doubt that his mother's faith made a deep impression on Fulton's spiritual formation. Her daily reading of the Bible, her nightly recitation of the rosary and her weekly invitations to priests to join the Sheen family for dinner all made Scripture and prayer as natural a part of life as eating, drinking and breathing. Perhaps those dinner guests too provided the catalyst for young Fulton to prepare spiritual talks. Even as a child he was known to entertain visitors with an occasional religious discourse as his mother looked on with pride.[9]

Once Fulton plucked a flower from a geranium plant that was for sale outside of a grocery store. Delia grew geraniums on her windowsill, and her son thought he would "help" her out by adding another to her "garden." When Fulton presented the offering to his mother, she was not as pleased as he had anticipated. In fact, she interrogated him. Once she found out that he had stolen it and from where, she marched him right over to his piggy bank and demanded he shake out fifty cents to give to the grocer, Mr. Madden.

Fulton protested: Fifty cents! The plants were being sold for only ten cents, and he had only stolen the *flower* from one! Nevertheless, his mother explained to him, there was such a thing as "restitution," and he was going to learn what that was. He was making up for his crime, not just the worth of the plant. When Fulton returned to the store, however, the compassionate grocer sent him home with two geranium plants.[10]

It was Delia who fostered what would become Fulton's lifelong devotion to the Blessed Virgin Mary. She consecrated her firstborn son to the Blessed Mother by laying him on the altar of St. Mary Church on the day he was baptized.[11]

Unaware that his mother had done this, Fulton would later dedicate himself to the Virgin Mary at his own confirmation at the age of twelve, committing himself to a daily recitation of the Litany to the Virgin Mary, a practice he would continue for the rest of his life. He even took the name of the beloved disciple, John, for while hanging from the cross, Jesus had instructed John to take Mary into his home as his mother (see John 19:26–27). Fulton took this passage to heart and on his confirmation day became Fulton "J." Sheen.[12]

THE PROBLEM OF PRIDE
Fulton craved parental approval. While he earned prizes, medals and holy cards for his good performance at school, he rarely received praise from Delia and Newt. There was an occasional "well done" from his mother but nothing from his father. One day Fulton asked his mother why his father never said anything. She explained that his father did not want to spoil his son but added, "He is telling all the neighbors."[13]

This lack of praise while growing up may have helped or hindered Fulton in his lifelong struggle with vanity. Fulton would later reflect that "praise often creates in us a false impression that we deserve it."[14] Well aware that the weakness of pride was the thorn in his side, this knowledge would help Sheen cooperate with the Lord's work to transform his weakness into humility. He believed that true saintliness lay in a person's ability to admit his sinfulness and to allow God to forge a virtuous soul from his flawed one.

He used Saint John the apostle as an example: "In the New Testament, the character most often praised for charity is John.... But John was not always so loving.... At some time or other in John's life, he *seized* upon the weak spot of his character—upon his want of kindness to his fellow man—and through cooperation with Grace he became the greatest Apostle of Charity."[15]

Fulton would have his first and last case of stage fright while leading the rosary at a school assembly. After attending Spalding Institute, he enrolled in St. Viator College, where it was customary to have a different student each day lead the rest of the school in this prayer to Our Lady. On Fulton's day to lead the prayer, which was held in the gymnasium, he became so nervous about halfway through that he could not continue.

Tellingly, the reason for his anxiety was rooted in pride and not humility. Fulton was distracted from prayer when he looked across the gym and noticed the stage being set up for that night's debate. He was on the debate team, and he began thinking about the debate and lost track of his prayer. (He and his partner won that evening's debate.)

Throughout his life Fulton Sheen would find his pride put to the test.

THE CALL
"A vocation is so very sacred that one does not like to speak of it," Sheen once wrote.[16] Although he knew he was called

MEET FULTON SHEEN

to be a priest from a young age, for years he chose not to share this knowledge with anyone else. Instead, like Mary, he pondered it in his heart.

Sheen once described what the call to the priesthood felt like: "For the most part, a religious vocation is rather a silent but insistent whisper, yet one that demands a response; no violent shaking of bedposts or loud noises in the night. Just, 'you are called to be a priest.'"[17] It was a gentle persistence; a nudge; a knowing.

Even though he desired the priesthood, when the call came he would sometimes try to "drive it out of...[his] mind only to have it come back again."[18] He almost postponed his entrance into the seminary, and doing so could have sent his life in an entirely different direction. Sheen recalled this incident as "a turning point in my life."[19] Obedience saved him.

It was the summer after Sheen had finished college. He won a three-year university scholarship worth close to ten thousand dollars. Thrilled that his pursuit of a Ph.D. would be fully funded, he dashed over to St. Viator's College to tell the good news to his friend and supporter Father William J. Bergan. Finding the priest on the tennis court, Sheen cried out, "Father Bergan, I won...!"

Father Bergan stopped what he was doing, walked over to Sheen and took him by the shoulders. Instead of pulling him into an embrace of congratulations, however, he looked Fulton in the eye and said, "Do you believe in God?"

When Sheen said he did, Bergan persisted. He didn't mean theoretically, he meant for real. Sheen had to be honest. "I *hope* I do."

"Tear up the scholarship.... You know you have a vocation; you should be going to the seminary."

Sheen argued that he could still enter the seminary *after* receiving his doctorate.

"Tear up the scholarship; go to the seminary," Bergan insisted. "This is what the Lord wants you to do.... Do it, trusting in Him."

Called to an act of faith, Sheen felt the paper tear under his own hands. "I have never regretted that decision," he said later.[20]

A STUDIOUS PRIEST

On September 20, 1919, Fulton Sheen was ordained a priest. On this day he resolved to offer the Holy Eucharist every Saturday in honor of the Blessed Mother, in hopes of soliciting her protection for his priesthood. He also resolved to make a Holy Hour before the Blessed Sacrament each day for the rest of his life. He kept both of his resolutions without fail.

Once ordained, Fulton was sent to the Catholic University in Washington to earn his doctorate in philosophy. He studied there for two years but felt he needed a greater challenge. He was especially interested in learning how best to "answer the errors of modern philosophy in the light of the philosophy of St. Thomas."[21] For this he was sent to Louvain, the university Bishop Spalding had prophesied he would attend.

Father Sheen did exceedingly well in his studies. He received his Ph.D. in July 1923 and was then invited to work towards the *agrégé*. The name of this honor means "sum total," which describes the kind of knowledge one needed to possess in order to earn it. In fact, once a person received this distinction, he was automatically eligible to join, or be "aggregated" to, the faculty of Louvain. Sheen accepted the invitation and went to Rome and London to study theology for about a year.

Upon his return to Louvain he took the oral examination, which required that he answer questions from professors of other universities for eight hours straight. There were four possible grades, and, according to tradition, the grade received would have a bearing on what beverage would be served at his congratulatory dinner. If it was the passing grade of "Satisfaction," water would be served. With "Distinction" came beer; with "Great Distinction," wine; with "Very Highest Distinction," champagne.

That evening it was champagne all around.

A TEST OF OBEDIENCE

With this impressive scholastic achievement, Sheen received two offers of prestigious teaching positions, one at Oxford and one at Columbia. The positions were of equal stature, and Sheen hardly knew which to choose. In his excitement he wrote to his bishop, Edmund M. Dunne, and asked which offer the bishop thought he should accept.

The bishop's reply was a surprise. He wanted neither for Sheen; he commanded instead that Fulton "come home."[22]

So Sheen flew back to the United States and reported for work in the crumbling parish of St. Patrick's in Peoria, Illinois. The neighborhood was poor and underdeveloped.

The church too was in disrepair and had a piddling number of parishioners, the majority of whom didn't even speak English. Some people considered it the worst parish assignment in the entire diocese. To top it off, despite all of his achievements, thirty-year-old Sheen was tapped to be not the pastor but rather the pastor's assistant, serving in the humble position of curate.

Nevertheless, Sheen fulfilled his role dutifully, making friends with the pastor and visiting every home in the parish. In no time at all the young priest's reputation for spiritually moving and educational sermons increased attendance at Mass, and the number of daily communicants grew from four to ninety. Priests in neighboring churches were dismayed to see attendance at their Masses diminish as their parishioners defected to St. Patrick's.

Editorials in the local paper complained that the bishop was wasting Sheen's obvious talents in a backwater church.[23] Sheen did not say a word against the bishop; instead he accepted his fate and simply saw to the needs of his parishioners. Indeed, miracles were happening.

On one eve of First Friday, a time set aside to hear confessions, a young woman entered the confessional without the least intention of confessing her sins. "I am here to kill time," she informed Father Sheen.

Believing her to be too ashamed to admit her sins, Sheen had a proposal: "If I could see you, I could probably make your confession for you. Will you let me take down this veil between us and turn on the light?"

The young woman, whose name was Agatha, agreed.

"You are a streetwalker," Sheen understood from looking at her. "That is your confession, is it not?"

"No," Agatha said, "there is something else."

Sheen pleaded with her for twenty minutes, but she would not divulge her sin. He spent another half hour on the front steps of the church asking her why she would not take part in the sacrament. Finally Agatha said, "I will tell you, and then I will leave."

She had been arrested for prostitution and sent to live with the Sisters of the Good Shepherd. In order to get away, Agatha had made a pact with the devil. "I promised… that I would make nine sacrilegious Communions if he would get me out of the home." On the ninth day she had managed to escape. After admitting this to Father Sheen, Agatha ran off into the night.

Sheen returned to the confessional, and he asked every penitent he heard the rest of the evening to say a rosary for the conversion of a sinner. Then he stayed up the rest of the evening praying at the communion rail. It was after midnight when the front door slowly opened and Agatha walked in, heading straight for the confessional. Sheen followed her and helped her to find God's forgiveness as a new day began.[24]

A NEW ASSIGNMENT

Father Sheen wasn't at St. Patrick's a year before he received a phone call from Bishop Dunne. "Three years ago I promised you to…the Catholic University as a member of the faculty," he informed a surprised Sheen. "Because of the success you had [in Europe], I just wanted to see if you would be obedient. So run along now; you have my blessing."[25]

Fulton's pride had been tested, and he had passed with flying colors!

Sheen would teach at Catholic University in Washington, D.C., for over twenty years. "I loved teaching," he would later write. "I loved it because it seemed so close to the prolongation of the Divine Word."[26] He also believed that "teaching is one of the noblest vocations on earth, for, in the last analysis, the purpose of all education is the knowledge and love of truth."[27]

Even though he was elected president of the American Catholic Philosophical Association, the governmental aspect of university life did not hold his interest. He much preferred that the college focus on the "primacy of the spiritual."[28] In fact, his lack of administrative skills would be a weakness he would carry into his years as director of the Society of the Propagation of the Faith.

Sheen more than made up for his limitations in this area with one of his strengths: public speaking. It was during his years at Catholic University that he began to be called on—and noticed for his talent—as a public speaker. He made a name for himself with a homily at a solemn pontifical Mass in the Basilica of the Immaculate Conception.

Sheen was more than happy to spend his weekends on the lecture circuit, accepting invitations to give a series of talks at churches in both Pittsburgh and New York. Demand for his appearances grew, and he began giving more talks outside of the classroom than inside. Finally the National Catholic Welfare Council approached Sheen with an opportunity to reach a larger audience than he ever had before. They asked him to preach the "electronic gospel,"[29] on radio.

❧ 2 ❧

A Priest Forever

"I DON'T KNOW WHY I EVER INVITED THAT MAN."[1]

That was the immediate reaction of Father Riley, a Paulist friar, as he listened to Father Sheen make his first live radio broadcast during the lenten season of 1928. The Paulist fathers had invited Sheen to give a series of Sunday evening sermons on the New York radio station WLWL ("We Listen, We Learn").[2] Another friar, Father Lyons, who knew Sheen from Rome, asked Riley to listen a bit longer. Thankfully, he did, and he heard enough to know he should ask Sheen back to speak on many other radio broadcasts.

There was already a "radio priest" at the time. Father Charles Coughlin had been on the air since 1926. An equal-opportunity offender of sorts, Father Coughlin was a very popular yet controversial figure whose theological talks could deteriorate into extremist personal views on political matters. Church officials eventually ordered the provocative personality to cease his radio broadcasts and serve out the rest of his days as a parish priest in Royal Oak, Michigan.

THE CATHOLIC HOUR

By 1930, Coughlin and his Protestant counterparts had stirred up enough dissention to inspire the Federal Communications Commission to call for non-fundamentalist religious programming. Both NBC and CBS responded by offering free time to Catholic, Protestant and Jewish groups. The National Council of Catholic Men, a branch of the National Catholic Welfare Council, decided to sponsor a new radio program called *The Catholic Hour* on radio station WEAF in New York.

Father Sheen's previous radio experience made him a perfect choice to appear as a guest speaker on the new radio program. He debuted with a twenty-minute talk on the evening of March 9, 1930, the second broadcast in the series' history. Sheen was so well-received that he became a regular speaker on the program.

In his early addresses Sheen was required to read from a script that had been approved by church officials. This was to avoid another Coughlin-like situation. The format of *The Catholic Hour* also allowed for a question-and-answer period, however, and it was there that Sheen's ability to come up with unrehearsed, intelligent replies was obvious. His storehouse of knowledge helped him to really shine.

Each week on *The Catholic Hour,* regular speakers and guest church officials discussed various Catholic topics, and the Paulist choir sang the best liturgical music of the time. The program received fan mail from all over the world, and the majority of it—anywhere from three to six thousand pieces a day[3]—was directed personally to Sheen. Even though he took up only twenty minutes of the show's hour of airtime, most people seemed to think that Fulton Sheen *was The Catholic Hour.*[4]

At the height of Sheen's popularity on the radio, approximately four million Americans were listening to his weekly broadcasts, and a third of them were not even Catholic.[5] Listeners all over the world were able to catch the program on their shortwave radios, and Fulton J. Sheen soon became an internationally recognized name. He was a star, not for his glory but for God's. He remained with *The Catholic Hour*—and was its strongest draw—for over twenty years.

ROME RESPONDS

Since his days at Louvain, Sheen had been writing scholarly spiritual books. He was up to three published works by the time he made it to radio. Once he began to regularly broadcast the word of God into the home of the average American citizen, a change came over his writing "voice." He began using a more accessible yet still beautiful style and tone in his writings. His books essentially became evolved and expanded versions of his radio addresses. This allowed him to churn out twice the number of publications he had previously.

Sheen's radio broadcasts proved so popular and yet so orthodox that in 1934 the pope elevated Sheen's status to that of "papal chamberlain." This title confers upon its bearer membership in the papal household. Sheen could now be called "Monsignor." This lasted for just a year, because in 1935 Sheen was elevated yet again, this time to a domestic prelate. He could then be addressed by the even longer and more impressive "Right Reverend Monsignor Fulton J. Sheen."

A "Right Reverend Monsignor" had to look the part, and so appeared the long purple cape (which is called a *ferraiola*), black cassock and red sash that would become part of the Fulton Sheen uniform. Some young boys once shouted out "Superman" when they saw him on stage from across the street.[6]

In his confessional autobiography Sheen would write, "When I was a priest I thrilled at being called 'Father.' I found the title 'Monsignor' mellifluous.... I loved creature comforts. I dressed well and I excused myself for this, saying that the ambassador of Christ should always present himself as a gentleman to the people and one of whom they could be proud.... This can be overrationalized."[7]

Sheen was perhaps being a bit hard on himself. Those who knew him personally agree that the Sheen one saw in public was the Sheen one saw in private. There were no stories of a "secret" side to him. Even his enjoyment of his priestly regalia was not hidden and was perhaps a sign not so much of his pride as of true happiness in his vocation.

Publicly and privately Sheen was a learned, charming and energetic man. However, the quality that most seemed to draw his audience was the strength of his convictions. His listeners could tell that he truly and passionately believed what he preached.

OVERWORK

Sheen's tendency to work too hard landed him in the hospital twice in the early 1940s as he required medical care and bed rest.

While he was still stationed in Washington, D.C., letters responding to his weekend radio addresses in New York revealed an avid interest in Catholic instruction. Sheen offered to teach classes himself. He began shuttling between Manhattan and Washington, D.C. twice a year in order to instruct adults in catechism, which he called "convert classes," for blocks of time. It took anywhere from twenty to twenty-five hours of study with Sheen for his students to be received into the church.

The classes began small, but enrollment soon increased, which necessitated a larger classroom. Sheen noted, "These classes were first held in the rectory of the cathedral, in St. Patrick's Cathedral School and later on in a small auditorium."[8]

Back in Washington, D.C., fellow priests thought Sheen was stretching himself too thin. They warned him that he was on the path to burnout or even death before the age of forty-five. But Sheen was undaunted. He had been blessed with an incredible amount of energy: he didn't walk as much as bound up a flight of stairs. His experience had proven to him that God replaced whatever he gave away in time, energy and money.

One Sunday, however, Sheen felt ill, and it was discovered that he was burning with a 102-degree fever.[9] He preached at St. Patrick's anyway. Later that evening, against the advice of his doctor, Sheen fulfilled his broadcast duties on *The Catholic Hour*. Soon he was hospitalized with a severe case of influenza. Apparently he did not learn his lesson, for he would check into the hospital a year later, due again to overwork.

Each time he recovered Sheen would continue at his zealous pace. He could not resist the urge to feed the spiritual hunger of his students, who included housewives, alcoholics, college students, beggars and businessmen. He found it pure joy to watch each group change once they came to know Jesus. He saw people who had previously sought out the best seats in the room turn and offer those places to others instead. The spirit of charity, generosity and acceptance would eventually take over, and Christ could be found in the midst of them.

A DISCERNING EYE

Just as Bishop Spalding had recognized the seeds of a priestly vocation in Fulton, Sheen was able to do the same for others once he became a priest. In fact, he believed God gave some priests this particular gift of spiritual discernment.[10]

Once, when Fulton was already an elderly bishop, he was walking down the aisle of a church in the diocese of Rochester when he noticed a young boy. Something about the boy drew his attention, and the bishop asked him if he had ever considered becoming a priest.

"I sometimes pray for it."

Sheen encouraged him. "I am sure you have a vocation; continue to pray to our Blessed Mother that you may be strengthened in it."

Sometime later the young man wrote to the bishop to let him know that he had joined the Jesuits.[11]

On an earlier occasion the bishop celebrated the midnight Mass in Washington, D.C., and remained afterward to greet the crowd that had gathered outside to exchange Christmas greetings. It was 1960. Among the many people congregated there, Fulton found his gaze zeroing in on an African American boy and his father standing at the edge of the crowd. He called the boy forward and asked, "Young man, do you ever think of becoming a priest?" The boy answered that he did, and the bishop laid his hands on his head and said a prayer for him.

When he had finished praying over the young man, the father wanted to know what had just happened between the priest and his son. When Sheen told him, the father was joyous. He excitedly told the bishop that ever since his son's birth he had prayed constantly that he would have a vocation to the priesthood. Sheen never found out whether or not that boy became a priest, but he had hope.[12]

There is a distinction between a career and a vocation. One is work, and the other is what a person is made for. A vocation is not a rung on the corporate ladder or a stepping-stone toward some other job in the future; nor is it chosen because it fits in with one's social work aspirations and desire to change the world. Sheen wrote in his autobiography, "No true vocation starts with 'what I want' or with 'a work I would like to do.'… If society calls, I can stop service; if Christ calls, I am a servant forever."[13]

Sheen saw three stages to a calling:

1. The first was an awakening to the presence of God and to his holiness. One needn't be struck down as Saint Paul was, Sheen said, nor hear the voice of God like the rumble of thunder. What happens is more like a shift in the person's perception. One begins to recognize and acknowledge in a new way the presence of that Holy Other.

2. The second stage is a sense of unworthiness. When a person becomes newly aware of God and his glory, suddenly one sees too the nothingness one is in comparison. This was a good and necessary stage, Sheen believed, as a humble person is one whom the Lord can work with. If a person feels that he deserves God's attention or has somehow earned it, then this pride will prevent his heart from hearing what the Lord wishes to say to it.

The bishop was well aware that "[God] did not call angels to be priests, he called men."[14] It is often hard to be truly humble, and most of us have to undergo trials that help to purge us from our sins. This purification process never really ends. It can take on many forms in a person's lifetime, such as, "mental anguish, betrayals, scandals, [and] false accusations."

3. The last stage is the response, which is entirely up to the person called. We all have free will.[15]

PRESERVING VOCATIONS

Sheen sometimes could tell when a young man would *not* be a priest, and for a period of about five years in the late sixties, he had the uncomfortable ability to spot the priest who would leave his vocation. The key to recognizing such a priest was what the bishop discerned to be an opposition to Christ.

It was a time of great upheaval in the church, right after Vatican II. Sheen was preaching many retreats for priests—work he enjoyed immensely. He discovered that when he spoke on subjects such as social justice, sex, psychology or some other trendy topic of the time, he would be well received. Once he began speaking on Christ, however, he would notice maybe two or three priests becoming restless and uncomfortable. He would not be surprised—although he would be deeply saddened—when these priests would later leave the priesthood.

He was not surprised because he had noticed that in the Gospel of John right after he introduced the challenging doctrine of the Eucharist (see John 6:35–71), Jesus announced that one of his disciples would betray him. Judas would be the first one to leave the table where the Eucharist was instituted at the Last Supper (John 13:21–30).[16]

Sheen felt wounded by every loss, once confessing, "The knowledge of a consecrated man of God or a consecrated woman abandoning her vows always caused a heartbreak in my soul."[17]

Sheen eventually perceived a pattern to the falling away of a priest from his vocation. It was so consistent that he could not ignore it. He recorded the stages in hopes of bringing them to the attention of his fellow priests and helping them to avoid losing their call.

Neglect of prayer was the first step. Once a priest abandoned prayer, he was sure to tumble down the remaining steps.

The second step was moving away from the Eucharist. Sheen once wrote, "A priest who would say: 'I am on vacation, so I don't read Mass' has already confused vocation with vacation."[18]

The third step was the pursuit of a comfortable life. Then came the fourth step, which was following the allurement of pleasure. At this point the priest begins to place himself in the way of temptations that he knows he is not equipped to resist. Without prayer to fortify him, it is small wonder that he is not strong enough.

By the time he reaches this last step, the priest has completely fallen. He is substituting Christ and his place in the priest's life with one of God's creatures. This could be a relationship, an addiction or any person, situation or activity to which the priest now gives precedence over God, therefore making of it a false idol.[19]

This happens, Sheen felt, because priests forget that they are called to be victims. Or if they do remember, they are running away from the cross. Before Jesus came, all priests, be they pagan or Jewish, offered up a sacrifice distinct from themselves. When Jesus offered up his sacrifice, he was both the priest *and* the victim. Priests who came after Jesus, Sheen said, were called to be victims *with* Christ.

Sheen found the motto for this one day while in a private audience with Pope Paul VI. He watched the pontiff scrawl on a piece of paper, *Nolo sine cruce crucifixum,* or, "I do not wish to be crucified without a cross." Later, when the pope cleared off his desk and threw the paper away, Sheen asked permission to retrieve it from the garbage can and later had it framed.[20]

Sheen described the cross of the priest in his autobiography: "Each priest is crucified on the vertical beam of the God-given vocation and on the horizontal beam of the simple longing of the flesh."[21]

The renewal and sanctification of the priesthood was the key to the reform of the Catholic church and the salvation of the world, Sheen believed. To truly consecrate oneself to God was a constant act, not a one-time taking of vows in a public ceremony. The best way Sheen found to do this was through the setting aside of an hour each day for eucharistic adoration.

THE HOLY HOUR

"It is impossible to explain how helpful the Holy Hour has been in preserving my vocation," Sheen wrote in his autobiography. "A priest begins to fail in his priesthood when he fails in his love of the Eucharist."[22]

Sheen was quick to point out that keeping the Holy Hour did not prove that he was a *holy* priest, however. He knew there were sure to be saintly priests all over the world who could not or did not pray in adoration before the Blessed Sacrament with the same frequency that he did. In fact, Sheen felt that this personal daily act of devotion may have been more necessary for him than for others. He described it as being like "an oxygen tank,"[23] helping him "keep step"[24] with his fellow holy priests.

Also, as a self-disciplined person, ritual and routine were ways Sheen felt comfortable expressing his fidelity to God. And faithful he was. He kept his daily Holy Hour for over six decades.

While the Holy Hour is an act of one's devotion to God, it is not a devotional prayer, like a chaplet. Neither is it to be taken up as a hobby, like "spiritual knitting." "It is a sharing in the work of redemption," Sheen wrote.[25] "The Eucharist is…essential to our one-ness with Christ."[26] He believed that the Holy Hour was necessary for authentic prayer[27] and served three main purposes:

1. The first purpose was to combat Satan. Sheen noted that references to an "hour" in the New Testament were almost always connected to the devil, and he counted seven such references in the Gospel of John (see John 4:21; 7:30; 11:9; 12:23, 27; 16:32; 19:27). In the Garden of Gethsemane Jesus asked his apostles to stay awake with him one hour in preparation for his crucifixion. Even this was an hour of evil—the time of Judas' betrayal—and Jesus grieved over what must come to pass. By inviting his disciples to stay and support him in prayer, Jesus was offering them the chance to unite themselves to him as victim and do battle with Satan. It was an hour of reparation.

2. The second purpose of the Holy Hour was to give Jesus the one thing he asked his apostles to give him and which they failed to do: an hour of companionship. Although

Sheen saw the Holy Hour as supporting Christ as he did combat with the devil, he didn't see it as an *action*. Rather it was remaining at the side of Christ; it was showing him companionship and love.

The person observing the Holy Hour might have to make a sacrifice—such as missing a television show, going without an extra hour of sleep or forgoing some other kind of pleasure—with the sole purpose of keeping Jesus company for one hour instead. Sheen knew that sacrifice was not something Americans did easily. He wrote in his book *Peace of Soul*, "In this world most of us mind pain more than we do sin; in fact, we often believe pain to be the greater evil." This was why the Holy Hour was something to be undertaken willingly and not out of some kind of felt obligation. Sheen warned, "Unless there is love, sacrifice...will be felt as an evil."[28]

3. The third purpose became obvious over time. The more often a person prayed his Holy Hour, the more like Jesus that person became, because all three purposes served the one main purpose of encouraging a deep, personal encounter with Christ.

Sheen felt that the effort of keeping up the practice of the Holy Hour was nothing compared to the rewards he reaped from it. And it was an effort. A friend once paid a call on Sheen only to have the priest rush through the visit so that Sheen could fit his Holy Hour into an already hectic schedule.[29] To avoid this type of scenario, Sheen advised that the best time to make a Holy Hour was "early, before the day sets traps for us."[30]

Another time, in Chicago, Sheen went to a church and asked the pastor for permission to pray before the Blessed Sacrament. It was after seven in the evening, so the priest unlocked the church, let Sheen in and left, letting the door lock behind him. After one hour in prayer before the Lord, Sheen spent two more hours trying to devise a means of escape from the church. He finally found a small window he could jump out of, and ended his adventure landing in a coal bin.[31]

Sheen once found himself in Paris with just an hour to spare. He entered the Church of St. Roch and, after a prayer of adoration, sat down to meditate, only to fall asleep. Exactly one hour later he woke up. Somewhat embarrassed, Sheen asked God if a Holy Hour had been made. He believed that his angel replied, "Well, that's the way the Apostles made their first Holy Hour in the Garden, but don't do it again."[32]

When he wasn't traveling, it was easier for Sheen to keep his commitment. Over the years, in the various apartments he lived, he always had a room converted into a chapel. He had special permission from the Vatican to keep the Blessed Sacrament reserved in his home and was therefore able to say Mass and keep his Holy Hour every day.[33]

Sheen also did his work before the Blessed Sacrament. He wrote his speeches and his autobiography in the presence of the One who always gave him the most inspiration: Christ in the Eucharist.

Promoting the Holy Hour was something Sheen felt comfortable doing because he practiced it successfully himself. To encourage it all the more, he produced booklets explaining this prayer method, with a guide to help readers make their own Holy Hour. He persuaded laypeople that this was a type of prayer available to everyone, not just to priests and religious.

A SPIRITUAL FAMILY

Sheen held the laity in high esteem, once remarking, "Mind my words,...the laity will save the Church in the United States."[34] The laity can also save priests in their struggles with loneliness—to which diocesan priests are particularly prone, as they lack the benefits of a supportive religious community. Even Jesus surrounded himself with friends. Of course, being alone and being lonely are not the same thing. And even a married person in the company of a big, loving family can suffer from loneliness.

Sheen was known to keep to himself; and as a celibate priest with his own apartment, he experienced many moments of solitude. In fact, he may have had a preference for it. Yet people were of primary concern to him, and he would sacrifice his privacy when he saw the need to do so. He enjoyed socializing and made many friends, though his intimate ones were few. He often would remain friends with a person for life. Sometimes Sheen befriended entire families.

One such family was the Cahills. Vincent Cahill was an FBI agent, and while Sheen had connections with the Federal Bureau of Investigation, it was Vincent Cahill's wife, Marian, who made contact with Sheen. The woman first reached out to the priest when she was pregnant and in great distress because her five-year-old daughter,

Suzanne, was dying of leukemia. Marian did not know how she and her husband were going to cope with their loss. She wrote to Sheen.

Immediately upon receiving her letter, then Bishop Sheen invited the family to the headquarters of the Society of the Propagation of the Faith, which he was heading at that time. He showered them with gifts of religious articles, including a heavy medal of Saint Christopher, a World Mission rosary, a statue of the Blessed Mother, an ivory crucifix and, for little Suzanne, an ivory rosary and gold ring. He also gave them all special blessings.

The Cahills found consolation and strength in this forty-five-minute visit with Bishop Sheen. Marian would later call him a "vivid picture of a true, living Christ."[35]

A few months later Suzanne passed away. Sheen immediately wrote to extend his sympathy and prayers to the family. The Cahills and Sheen continued to correspond, and eventually letters turned into invitations and invitations into visits. The Cahills visited Sheen on the set of his television show, *Life Is Worth Living,* and in his Manhattan apartment, and Sheen visited the Cahills at their residences in the Bronx and Yonkers.

The Cahill children eventually numbered ten, and one of the boys was christened Fulton John. Sheen remained involved in their lives and was active in their spiritual development. He was often a pivotal participant in their reception of the sacraments, baptizing five of them, presiding at the marriages of three and, as bishop, confirming seven.

One Christmas season, at a time when he was on television on a weekly basis and had already achieved a considerable amount of fame, Sheen visited the family at the home of Marian's mother. He surprised the two oldest Cahill boys with gifts of brand new bicycles. The boys excitedly took them out for a spin as Fulton watched with delight.

As the family trooped home, Sheen noticed that the wheel on one of the bicycles needed adjusting. He asked Vincent to get him a wrench, then he crouched in the hallway of the apartment building and set to work. At that moment a neighbor who had been out drinking stepped off the elevator. He briefly took in the sight of the familiar-looking figure in the homburg hat and overcoat struggling in the corner, then continued on to his apartment. The next day he told Mr. Cahill that he was sure he drank too much the night before. He could have sworn he saw Bishop Sheen in the hallway fixing a bicycle.[36]

Some people see pink elephants; others, Fulton Sheen with a bicycle.

SPIRITUAL CHILDREN

Another way Sheen filled his need for family was by spiritually adopting his brothers' children. Joan Sheen was the daughter of his brother Joe, a bright and amiable girl. She later remembered her famous uncle as her "second father." As a child, she and her family often visited his New York apartment and always attended his radio broadcasts. On one special occasion the family had the treat of flying to California and attending a dinner party, where Joan met two of her uncle's biggest fans, screen stars Loretta Young and Irene Dunne.[37]

Another niece, Eileen Sheen, the daughter of his brother Tom, joined her uncle's tour of Europe one summer. She was nineteen, the perfect age to enjoy the educational and adventurous opportunity of touring England, Ireland, Italy, Spain, France and Belgium. The trip included meeting up with family in Ireland and an audience with the pope in Rome. It was mostly a whirlwind tour of meeting after meeting for Fulton, but Eileen enjoyed watching the warm reception he received wherever they went. She also admired his work ethic, noting that he kept up a writing schedule and meditated regularly.[38]

Fulton made sure the girls received proper schooling, and for this he looked to Rosemont College, a woman's institution located just outside Philadelphia. It had been fairly new when, in 1928, the young Father Fulton Sheen offered to lead a retreat for the religious sisters there in place of a Jesuit who had cancelled at the last minute.

When Sheen arrived at the front door for that retreat, the nuns first mistook him for an altar boy.[39] This was not the first time this had happened. Fulton had been ordained a priest at the tender age of twenty-four. Slender and small in frame, when he buttoned his coat over his Roman collar, he appeared younger than his years. On one occasion as a new priest, he knocked on the door of a sacristy, and the very monsignor who had invited him took one look at the figure standing before him in the rain and told him to go join the rest of the altar boys in the church.

Sheen won fans for life when he led the retreat for the community of the Sisters of the Holy Child Jesus and their foundress, Mother Mary Cleophas. He was just as impressed with them and their work of providing a solid education to young ladies, so he offered to fund a scholarship for deserving young women every year. This scholarship provided for the college educations of his two nieces as well as Jeanne Cahill.

Sheen, always one to be deeply invested in his commitments, visited the college almost annually. For nearly fifty years he served the school during these visits in some priestly capacity, be it leading a retreat or giving an address to the students.[40]

FRIENDS IN LONDON

Sometimes it was children who adopted Sheen. One cold November evening in London, he met five-year-old Ann O'Connor after a Benediction service at Notre Dame Church. The two chatted briefly and found that they had an Irish background in common. Ann invited the priest to her flat for tea at 3:00 PM the next day. Sheen accepted.

When Ann told her parents that she had invited a priest to tea, they didn't believe her. She was prone to fantasy, and perhaps her description of his wearing a "fur coat" (instead of his having a fur collar on his coat) made him sound even more like a figment of her imagination.

Ann was undaunted, and the next day she prepared her tea. She watched for the arrival of her guest from the cold of her balcony. At three o'clock on the dot, Sheen made his appearance, rewarding her faith with a giant box of sweets, which Ann still remembered when recalling that visit nearly eighty years later.

Sheen became friends with the entire O'Connor family, and whenever he was in London he never failed to call on them. The O'Connors made it to America as well, visiting Sheen six times. They corresponded regularly over many years, leaving Ann with a treasure trove of two hundred letters, which she prized highly.[41]

In a retreat he once gave for priests, Sheen explained that priests may be celibates, but they "are not to be barren." "God hates sterility," he proclaimed, but not in a literal sense. Everyone, he said, was called to a fertility of spirit.

In the Old Testament priests were literally married in order to produce physical progeny. But since the establishment of the church, their progeny was to be of a spiritual nature. On Judgment Day, Sheen warned the priests at one retreat, "God will ask you, 'Where are your children?'"[42]

The vocation of everyone, man or woman, married or single, priest or layperson, was to be like Mary: that is, through God's grace, to lovingly and humbly conceive and bear Christ within and then usher him in service to one another.

❦ 3 ❧

The Blessed Mother

"LET THOSE WHO THINK THAT THE CHURCH PAYS TOO much attention to Mary give heed to the fact that Our Blessed Lord gave ten times as much of His life to her as He gave to His Apostles," Fulton Sheen is quoted as saying.[1] He was a great defender of the Virgin Mary as well as an apologist for misunderstood Catholic doctrine about her. "The Church has never adored Mary, because only God may be adored," he explained in his autobiography. "But she, of all creatures, was closest to God."[2]

Sheen knew that God, of course, could be close to anyone. Often the Lord chose to connect with an individual through the gifts he had given them. Some people were close to God through the intellect. They were very knowledgeable about God, possessing a noticeable wisdom and understanding of his mind. Others God reached through the will. These people were "in sync" with God's will and ready to sublimate their own will in favor of God's. Still other people were connected to God through their bodies. They expressed this connection through personal purity, fasting and other corporal challenges.

What made Mary so special, Sheen noted, is that she was close to God in all three of these ways. Of all people she was closest to God in mind, will and body, which is why God chose her to be his mother.[3]

ILLUMINATED BY THE SON

Sheen was familiar with the Protestant concern that Catholics equated Mary, a mere human, with Jesus, both man and God. He wished to make clear that this was not so. Comparing Mary to Jesus would be like calling the moon the sun, he said. The moon can never "take away from the brilliance of the sun." In fact, the moon has no light of its own. Its perceived beauty and light are only reflections of the sun's light and just the merest fraction of its brilliance.

"Mary reflects her Divine Son, without Whom she is nothing. On dark nights we are grateful for the moon; we see it shining, we know there must be a sun. So, in this dark night of the world, when men turned their backs on Him Who is the Light of the World, we look to Mary to guide our feet while we await the sunrise."[4]

Sheen saw this beautifully illustrated once at the Abbey of Gethsemani, a monastery in Kentucky, where he was conducting a retreat for Trappist monks. It was time for night prayers in the chapel. The voices of the monks—some two hundred strong—rose as one, singing the office as the chapel gradually grew darker and darker. As this was happening, Sheen noticed that the large, stained-glass window above the altar, which depicted the Blessed Mother surrounded by angels and saints, was growing brighter and brighter.

Finally, as the monks began the *Salve Regina,* a hymn to the Virgin Mary, the window shone its brightest, blazing due to the illumination of the setting sun. Sheen knew that just as the sun made the moon shine, the Son was the reason for the radiance of the Mother.[5]

When Sheen became a bishop, the motto he chose for his coat of arms was *Da per matrem me venire* or "Grant that I may come to thee through Mary."[6] From a young age Sheen had entrusted himself to the tender care of the Blessed Mother, secure in the knowledge that God had entrusted her with the care of his own Son. He relied on her guidance, knowing that she would lead him well in the way of obedience, as his own mother, Delia, had taught him by her faithful example.

In dedicating his priesthood to Mary, Sheen knew that he could count on her prayers, which God could never refuse since they could never go against his will. Finally, by building a relationship with Our Lady that honored her role as the Mother of God, it was his desire that she would recommend him to her beloved Son. Thus when his time on earth had passed and the Lord summoned him for judgment, Christ would "say...in His Mercy: I heard My Mother speak of you."[7]

MODEL OF CELIBACY

In a retreat he gave to priests later in his life, Fulton provided another reason why paying the proper respect to Mary was important: in her perfect obedience and virginity, she was a model and a safeguard for the priestly vow of celibacy.

From Adam and Eve to the wedding of the Lamb in the Book of Revelation, the Scriptures were built around a theme of nuptials, Sheen said. The story of the relationship of humanity to God was the story of an unfaithful spouse to a perfect and loving one. Devotion to Mary was an act of fidelity to God. Jesus was the new Adam and Mary the new Eve. Since Jesus was the Bridegroom and Mary a symbol of the church, a priest could dedicate himself to Mary in imitation of the Bridegroom's commitment to his church.

Consecration to the Blessed Mother, Sheen explained, helps negate attachments to other women, which can distract a priest from devoting himself to the church as his spouse. It works in much the same way as a husband's vow to his wife helps to prohibit his attaching himself to other intimate relationships with women. Sheen had noticed that when there was a "decline in celibacy,... purity,... [and] the sanctity of marriage," there was sure to be a "decline in devotion to the Blessed Mother."[8]

Marriage and celibacy do not contradict one another. In fact, the vocation of marriage and the vocation of celibacy, properly lived, support one another. Sheen believed that the two ways of life shared the same desires and motivations, such as the pursuit of everlasting love and the sacrifice of forsaking all others in order to somehow achieve it. Ultimately, God and love were one and the same.

While celibacy can be a challenge at times, Sheen warned that the challenges could increase due to certain attitudes or circumstances. The attitude that celibacy is a matter of willpower or the belief that it is a gift one gives to the church can both make celibacy difficult because they are wrong. The truth is that celibacy is a gift *from* God that is to be received, "much as a girl may receive a proposal."[9]

Celibacy becomes its most challenging when the person who has accepted the gift falls out of love with its giver. Then celibacy becomes a "great burden," since "once our passions cease to burn for Him, they begin to burn toward creatures." After all, Sheen pointed out, when a man is passionately in love with his wife, he has no desire to be unfaithful to her, whereas a man who constantly argues with his wife is more apt to look for a more agreeable alternative.[10]

Both matrimony and holy orders are equal in value in the eyes of God, since, ideally, entering into either one of these sacraments is an acceptance of a call from God. Each vocation has it pluses and minuses, however, with the obvious challenge of celibacy being loneliness. Yet the depth of sharing in the intimacy of loneliness with God could lead, as Sheen quotes Dag Hammarskjöld as saying, "to a communion closer and deeper than any achieved by two bodies."[11]

PRAYERS FOR THE BISHOP

"And someday you will be just as I am." The prophecy of Bishop Spalding came to pass on June 11, 1951, in the Church of St. John and St. Paul in Rome. There Fulton J. Sheen was ordained a successor to the apostles, a bishop of the church.

It had been a long wait. Sheen had wanted to be a bishop from almost the moment he was ordained a priest. While still studying in Louvain, Sheen prayed for this intention through the intercession of his special friend, the Virgin Mother.

It became something of a routine for Sheen to drop by the church of St. Michael before class. He would take a moment to stop at each of the paintings representing the seven sorrows of the Blessed Mother and pray a Hail Mary. The Virgin, he knew, could only pray for God's will to be done, so if it was the will of God, the bishopric would be his.

As a professor at Catholic University, young Sheen was tempted to have his dream fulfilled early. Bishop Kelly of Oklahoma City offered to submit Sheen's name to Rome for consideration for the bishopric. Fulton thought it over. His will, he discerned, might well be saying, "Yes," but he did not feel that God's will was in agreement. He wrote to Bishop Kelly: "There are two ways…one advances in the church…by a push from below…[or] by a gift from above."[12] Sheen wanted divine inspiration and not earthly ambition to influence the Holy See in their choice.

Years later Sheen was able to accept the honor with joy in his heart. Even after the Virgin Mother answered his prayer about his bishopric, Sheen could not bring himself to stop offering prayers on behalf of Mary's seven sorrows. Her loyalty deserved his in return.

Celebrating the feast days of Our Lady was a particular joy to Bishop Sheen. Near the end of his life, however, he noted that many of those celebrations had been times of great physical trial. On the feast of Our Lady of Mount

Carmel, July 17, 1977, he nearly died as he underwent emergency heart surgery. The following month, on the Feast of the Assumption, the bishop had a pacemaker implanted. A month later, on September 8, which the church celebrates as the birthday of the Virgin Mary, Bishop Sheen began suffering "tortures" from a kidney ailment that would last several weeks.

Reflecting on these afflictions, the bishop observed that like all good mothers, "the Blessed Mother not only gives sweets, but she also gives bitter medicine." He added, "If my own earthly mother laid me on her altar at birth, why should not my Heavenly Mother lay me at His Cross as I come to the end of life?"[13]

In fact, more than once Bishop Sheen expressed his desire to die on a Marian feast day or "on a Saturday which is dedicated to her,"[14] preferably in adoration before the Blessed Sacrament. Our Lady and the Eucharist were the two greatest devotions of his spiritual life.

LOURDES

One way Sheen liked to show his loyalty to Mary was by visiting her shrines. Whenever he was in Europe, he was sure to make a stop at either Fatima, in Portugal, or his personal favorite, the grotto in Lourdes, France. He would eventually visit Fatima about ten times and Lourdes about thirty.[15]

Every time he visited Lourdes, something remarkable happened. Sheen felt very close to Mary there and would converse with her as with a close friend.

On the fifth anniversary of his ordination to the priest-hood, Sheen decided to strike a deal with the Blessed Mother. Since he was still a university student, he was prac-tically penniless. He would use his last dime to get to Lourdes, but she would have to pay for his hotel bill so that he could stay there!

Upon arriving in Lourdes, Sheen secured a decent hotel room, feeling that the cheapest place would belie his faith and trust in Mary. Then he prayed a novena to the Blessed Mother. By the ninth day there was no sign from Our Lady, and his bill was due. The thought of being elbow-deep in dishwater flashed through his mind.

Finally, at ten in the evening, Sheen went back to the grotto to give Mary one last chance. There he met a man named Thomas Farrell, who asked him three questions: Are you an American priest? Do you speak French? And, what Sheen called "perhaps the most interesting question" he had heard in his life, have you paid your hotel bill? Farrell paid Sheen's bill and began a twenty-year friendship in the bargain.[16]

Sheen was in Lourdes again after finishing his univer-sity studies, awaiting his first assignment from Bishop Dunne. He worried that he would not see Europe for a long time—or perhaps ever again—and this would mean he would not see Lourdes again. He asked Mary for a sign that he would return someday. If her answer was "yes," he asked that before he left the shrine he would see a young girl, about the age of twelve, dressed in white, who would give him a white rose.

Sheen offered Mass at the shrine and prepared to leave, all the while keeping a lookout for his sign. As he headed toward the outer gate, he strained to see the sign, but no girl, no white, no rose. He prodded Mary to hurry, as he was running out of time. Then, just as he reached the outer gate, a white rose appeared, and holding it, a girl around the age of twelve, dressed all in white. The girl handed the rose to him. Sheen accepted the gift and left the grotto trembling.[17]

Without his sign from Mary, the hope of a return pilgrimage to Lourdes while working in a backwater parish in Peoria, Illinois, would have felt like a pipe dream. Because he had received his rose, however, Sheen wasn't worried. He even told the pastor that he intended to return to Lourdes in a year's time. Pastor Culleton doubted it very much. "I have been [here] for fifteen years and have not been to Europe once; as a curate, you expect to go at the end of the year?"

Sheen insisted it would happen, and a year later Bishop Dunne told Sheen to pack his bags. As he was being assigned to Catholic University in the fall, he would need the summer for further study in Europe.[18]

Sheen's experiences with the Blessed Mother taught him the value of faith. She often required him to hold on until the very last moment to get what he wished for. Had he failed to believe, he would have failed to receive any reward. Perhaps this is why he often ended his talks on the Blessed Mother by reciting a poem for children by Mary Dixon Thayer. It was entitled "Lovely Lady Dressed in Blue," and the last stanza is:

Lovely Lady dressed in blue
Teach me how to pray!
God was just your little Boy
And, you know the way![19]

Perhaps it was Our Lady who guided Sheen in his connection with the Carmelites. The bishop valued the deep contemplative prayer of the religious order. He found himself drawn to its charism, which taught awareness of one's sinfulness and the stripping of all false gods or inner barriers to holiness. This was a great help in his constant battle against pride.

Writing to the Carmelite nuns in New Albany, Indiana, Sheen asked for their prayerful support: "I want to cling…to Carmel for I love its love of Jesus.…Like the blind man of Jericho I shall go on shouting out to you continually to cure my blindness and my ills."[20]

The bishop, in turn, supported the order in the best ways he could. He used his formidable fundraising abilities to help provide for them. He traveled to Ireland on four separate occasions to celebrate Masses on Carmelite feasts and anniversaries. The special bond he formed with the order spanned more than five decades.

This personal love of Carmel went farther than admiration. In 1948, at the age of fifty-three, Fulton Sheen was professed as a Third Order Carmelite. The ceremony was conducted in the Carmelite House of Studies, Whitefriars Hall, in Washington, D.C. It was July 17, the day after the Feast of Our Lady of Mount Carmel.[21]

❧ 4 ❧

A Pioneer

FULTON J. SHEEN FOUND HIMSELF NEXT GOING WHERE no priest had gone before: to prime-time stardom.

"Radio," Sheen famously wrote in his autobiography, "is like the Old Testament, for it is the hearing of the Word without the seeing. Television is like the New Testament, for the Word is seen as it becomes flesh and dwells among us."[1]

In the early 1950s television executives decided it was time to bring to TV what Americans had been enjoying through the radio for years: religion. But how was this to be done? Could religion really go commercial?

A SHOW WORTH WATCHING
The Admiral Corporation provided the solution. It was not at all inappropriate for a manufacturer of television sets and radios to finance a television show—even a religious one. The company agreed to sponsor the program for a

season of twenty-six episodes at a cost of one million dollars. Sheen, with years of radio broadcasts under his belt, was tapped to star.

His television presentations would need to be more ecumenical than *The Catholic Hour*, in order to reach a wider audience. Sheen's talks would run the gamut of themes, such as psychology, politics, the arts and science. But no matter what topic he presented, he would argue his points skillfully from the Christian perspective and with a touch of humor.

Sheen would now be seen as well as heard all over the United States on the Du Mont network (later ABC). He would be earning the princely sum of twenty-six thousand dollars a show, which he always unhesitatingly handed over to the Society of the Propagation of the Faith, as he had resolved to refuse personal financial reimbursement for his services. In fact, the program itself would often serve as a platform for the Society and its mission work.

Life Is Worth Living, as the program was called, made its debut on February 12, 1952. The show was a first in many ways: a religious program on television, during prime time (Tuesday nights at 8:00 PM), sponsored by a corporation that would advertise on the air. Television itself was still in its infancy. Thankfully, the commercials were unobtrusive, playing only at the beginning and end of each episode.

The show was shot before a studio audience in New York's Adelphi Theatre. Its structure was simple but effective. Sheen, dressed in his bishop accoutrements, would stand in a set designed to look like the study of a rectory and speak on the topic of the evening as two to three cameras rolled. When presenting his points, he sometimes illustrated them on a chalkboard, the way a professor might when giving a lecture at a university. He never needed notes or cue cards.

His talks were typically about twenty-seven minutes long, and he would keep one eye on the clock as he spoke. A timekeeper on the set also would give him a tiny signal—the only one he requested—to let him know when he needed to wrap up his presentation. The bishop would conclude every talk at precisely the last minute he was allotted.

Sheen's natural professionalism cultivated wide-eyed admiration from people in the field. It seemed Fulton J. Sheen was made for TV. It wasn't watching the clock or getting the cue or even his uncanny abilities that helped him the most. Five minutes before each episode of his program, Sheen would stop everything and fall silent in prayer and recollection. "On television," Sheen would later admit, "I depended more on the grace of God and less on myself."[2]

GOD AT WORK

It could not have been anything but grace that made a success out of *Life Is Worth Living*. From the beginning there were many strikes against it. It was a little show, educational in format and initially carried only by two stations. Running against the bishop on the same night and time was NBC's *Texaco Star Theater*. What chance did a "show" that consisted solely of a priest looking directly into the camera and talking for half an hour have against the most popular show on TV?

Texaco Star Theater was an hour of wildly vaudevillian entertainment that made a superstar out of its leading player, Milton Berle. Movie houses and restaurants stood empty on Tuesday nights as people stayed home to watch Berle perform slapstick routines in outrageous costumes, such as when he famously dressed in drag. Berle and his antics were credited for the spike in television sales during the late forties and early fifties, and this earned him the nickname "Mr. Television." The American public affectionately dubbed him "Uncle Miltie," feeling that he was as comfortably familiar to them as a member of their own family.[3]

Meanwhile, CBS had scheduled its own counteroffensive to Milton Berle, starring the popular singer Frank Sinatra.

Yet, surprisingly enough, on the quieter Du Mont network, Bishop Sheen was quickly building an audience. He didn't talk down to his viewers, yet he didn't speak over their heads either. Soon seventeen stations were carrying *Life Is Worth Living*, then seventy-five stations. Almost overnight the show became a success, and then it became a sensation. In just two months Bishop Sheen was on the cover of *Time* magazine.

Sheen knew that the real star of the show was God. He was sure to begin and end his program with God as his focus.

One way he did this was by writing "J.M.J." on the chalkboard before writing anything else. These initials stood for the names "Jesus, Mary and Joseph." This was a habit he had adopted in kindergarten, when a nun taught him that he could bless his work in a special way by writing these initials on the top of his paper before writing anything else. Little did she know that by passing this custom along to Sheen, he would in turn promote it to two million viewers. Many of his Christian fans took up the practice.

Sheen would close his show with the words "God love you." This became a signature line for him, and he would later use it as the title of a column he wrote regularly for the Society of the Propagation of the Faith.

GOOD FOR A LAUGH

Had he been solely a pious figure, Sheen would never have received the audience and level of success he did. Milton Berle, it turned out, wasn't the only funny man on television. The bishop also became known for his ready sense of humor. He personally discussed the subject of humor with Berle on a number of occasions. Sheen believed that there was an undeniable relationship between it and faith.[4]

He made a rule of opening his talks with a joke or a funny story. The jokes were often self-deprecating in nature, as he was a great believer in humbling oneself to gain the trust of one's audience. A favorite he liked to tell was of an incident that happened on a boat trip across the Atlantic.

A deck steward approached Sheen and asked, "Are you the priest who preached the Mission Sunday sermon at St. Patrick's last year?"

Sheen answered, "Yes."

"I enjoyed every minute of that hour and a half," the steward said.

Sheen balked, claiming, "My good man, I never talked an hour and a half in my life."

The steward replied, "It seemed that long to me."[5]

Sheen also used humor to make a spiritual point or to provide a light moment when speaking on a heavy topic. In a talk on recognizing our own sinfulness, he mentioned how people can sin in small ways but fail to admit to themselves that they are doing wrong. In order for a person to admit to sin, however, he must first allow his conscience to speak to his heart. Sheen explained:

"There was a preacher once who was saying to the congregation, 'It is wrong to steal horses.' The congregation answered, 'Amen, amen.' 'It is wrong to steal cows.' 'Amen! Amen!' Then he said, 'It is wrong to steal chickens.' And someone shouted back, 'Now he is meddling.'"

After the laughter Sheen added, "Up to that point, conscience was not touched."[6]

Sheen could find humor even in the Scriptures. He once quipped, "It should be remarked in defense of all mothers-in-law that St. Peter remained the truest friend of Our Blessed Lord, despite the fact that Our Lord cured his mother-in-law."[7]

Sheen knew that humor helped keep his viewers interested. Another way to keep things moving along was having offscreen stagehands erase the notes he wrote on the chalkboard. This way Sheen could keep talking without interruption, and when he needed to write on the board again, he could return to a clean slate.

Since his television audience could not see how the chalkboard was erased, Sheen joked that he had the assistance of an angel named Skippy. After a while the ever-helpful "Skippy" became a staple of the show and a rather famous, if invisible, figure himself.

FATHER TELEVISION

The bishop was blessed with gifts that naturally attracted an audience: a combination of hypnotic charisma and telegenic looks that hooked viewers and then kept them watching. In a short time Sheen became a formidable and persuasive television personality.

Life Is Worth Living became so popular, in fact, that viewership for the first half hour of *Texaco Star Theater* fell. Instead of seeing the bishop as a rival, however, Milton Berle expressed only admiration and respect for Sheen. The Jewish comedian even became good friends with the cleric, whom he sometimes teasingly referred to as "Uncle Fultie."[8]

Another popular television star of the period, Jackie Gleason, also became a fan of the bishop. He would view tapings of *Life Is Worth Living* from the control booth. His admiration for Sheen, like Berle's, would transform into friendship. To commemorate his own fifty-first birthday, Gleason invited Sheen onto *The Jackie Gleason Show*. Greg Hildebrandt, who with his twin brother, Tim, would work for the bishop in the 1960s, recalled a framed photograph in Sheen's office known to be a personal favorite of the bishop. The photo showed Sheen embracing Jackie Gleason and grinning widely.[9]

In 1952 Fulton Sheen was nominated for an Emmy Award, the most prestigious television award given in the

United States. The category was "Most Outstanding Television Personality." Fellow nominees were television icons Lucille Ball and Edward R. Murrow and entertainers Jimmy Durante and Arthur Godfrey. It was Fulton Sheen who was the winner that year.

Caught somewhat off guard, Sheen found himself momentarily—and atypically—at a loss for words. Taking his cue from the acceptance speeches of the other recipients, he decided to give credit where credit was due. With a twinkle in his eye, he announced, "I wish to thank my four writers, Matthew, Mark, Luke and John."[10]

The recognition and awards did not stop there. The Advertising Club of New York awarded Sheen the title of "Our Television Man of the Year." Similarly, the *Radio and Television Daily* nationwide poll named him television's "Man of the Year." *Look* magazine recognized *Life Is Worth Living* as the best religious program in the United States not once, not twice, but three different times. The Catholic University Alumni Association presented Sheen with the Cardinal Gibbons Medal for his service to the Lord, America and his *alma mater* (in that order). That same year the Freedom Foundation of Valley Forge in Pennsylvania recognized Sheen and his program for contributing to the American way of life.

Sheen guest-starred on other television programs. In December of 1956 he and his fellow *Look* magazine award winners appeared on an episode of *The Toast of the Town* variety show, which later became *The Ed Sullivan Show*. He was also a "mystery guest" on the quiz show *What's My Line?*[11] The object of the game was to have blindfolded panelists guess the occupation of a guest, who was often famous and had to disguise his voice in an attempt to stump the players.

All this worldly praise and recognition did not go to Sheen's head, however. His cousin, Tom Holliger, who was staying with Sheen when the bishop won his Emmy, found the statuette the next morning. The bishop had left it standing on a steam radiator.

The tributes did not just come from his professional peers. Sheen received even more admiration from average men, women and children from all over the United States who watched his program, just as he had from his listeners when he was on the radio. Watching *Life Is Worth Living* became a weekly ritual for many.

Seeing Sheen and listening to him on a regular basis made his viewers feel that they could know and trust him on a personal level. People wrote to him as they would to an old friend. The bishop once estimated receiving as many as eighteen to twenty-five thousand letters a day.[12]

Fulton Sheen became a household name, and it led to the creation of other famous Sheens. One of the bishop's fans was a young Roman Catholic actor named Ramon Estevez. He was so inspired by Sheen that he wrote and asked permission to take his last name as part of his stage name. *Ramon* became *Martin,* and *Estevez* was changed to *Sheen.* Martin Sheen went on to become a successful movie and television star. His son Carlos also took the name Sheen, and as Charlie Sheen he has enjoyed recognition in both movies and television.

Because *Life Is Worth Living* was structured to be an ecumenical show, with educational and moral themes that were accessible to the general viewing audience, Sheen found that he received less hate mail from anti-Catholics and more letters of goodwill than he had when he was on the radio. Fulton stated that the majority of positive letters came from Jews, with Protestants coming second, and Catholics, surprisingly, coming in third.[13]

MISSIONARY MAN

The miracle of television was not the only way Sheen was able to travel around the world. Before *Life Is Worth Living*, Sheen had the opportunity to literally tour the world with the then archbishop of New York, Cardinal Francis Spellman.

Francis Spellman became archbishop of New York in 1939, despite media speculation that Fulton Sheen would be elevated to the post. Sheen was a favorite adopted son of the city and was considered "a real New Yorker" despite his Midwestern roots. He had a great love for the city and its people. New York City had become his home, having for him the intimacy of a small town despite its size and its position as the richest and most powerful diocese in the United States.

Spellman was also quite at home in the city. In 1946 he was further elevated to the status of cardinal. Well aware of Sheen's work on radio and the impact he was making on the listening world, Spellman saw much potential in Sheen for doing even bigger and better things in the church. In 1948 he invited Sheen to accompany him and a few other American bishops on a goodwill tour of the world. They would travel to Australia, China and Africa.

Although the two bishops shared similar attributes, such as being of Irish descent and truly orthodox Catholics, their styles and approaches differed. Spellman in his role as archbishop of New York City wielded great power and authority. He embodied a different kind of New Yorker than media star Sheen, who had more of the forces of intellect and personality at his disposal. Sheen was not the administrator Spellman was, and Spellman was not the learned orator Sheen was.

These similarities and differences worked to their advantage while on tour. With Spellman's position as the most powerful priest in the U.S. and Sheen's as the most influential one, their reception at some airports was akin to what musicians and movie stars receive today. Spellman took care of matters of diplomacy, and Sheen was handed most of the preaching duties.

And preach Sheen did. From the first day of the tour, he was tapped to address crowds of ten, twenty and sometimes even a hundred thousand. Almost every speech was recorded and broadcast on the radio later. Sheen was sometimes called on to speak publicly more than seven times a day. This prompted the cardinal to introduce Sheen at a ball in Melbourne with "This will be his ninety-ninth talk today."[14]

As the tour continued, Spellman came to rely on Sheen's oratory skill. He would begin a sermon and then "without any warning"[15] step aside and let Sheen finish the talk. Sheen began preparing to be unprepared.

By the time the tour stopped in Shanghai, Spellman noticed that Sheen was exhausted. Sheen was prone to overwork and rarely refused a request to speak publicly. Spellman ordered him not to accept any more speaking engagements without his permission.

Spellman also noticed that Sheen was far more popular than he had realized. Many people seemed to think Sheen had taken Spellman along on his trip, whereas the truth was the other way around. Often, after he celebrated a Mass, enthusiastic crowds mobbed Sheen for autographs. They were so zealous that Sheen needed bodyguards just to move through them.

Although Spellman received much the same treatment, there is a current belief that Spellman later grew to be jealous of Sheen. There was no evidence of this during the tour. In fact, in a speech in Sydney, Spellman announced that Sheen was "doing more than any archbishop or any bishop to make the Faith known and loved."[16] He even privately told Sheen how proud he was of all the hard work he was doing. And Sheen wrote in his journal that Spellman had absolutely no jealousy in him.[17] Despite their oil-and-water personalities, the two men of God managed to cooperate well under demanding circumstances.

Every country and every culture required different social graces. In his autobiography Sheen recalled the tribute a visiting Arab sheik once gave Spellman in Australia. He removed the eye from the lamb being served at dinner and offered it to the cardinal. Spellman heroically choked it down, then tactfully claimed to love it. The sheik, of course, then offered him the other eye.

The two clerics planted trees in Darwin, drank coffee in Java, read Mass in Singapore and visited wounded soldiers in a hospital in Manila. By the time they returned home, they had been gone fifty-two days and had covered forty-three thousand miles. Sheen's last entry in his travel journal was "Thank God."[18]

FEEDING THE HUNGRY

"A visit like ours...gives one an entirely different impression of the world, enlarges a point of view, develops a sympathy for others and makes one mission minded"[19] was another entry in Sheen's travel journal. His newly developed mission mind proved to be the perfect fit when the Vatican appointed him to be national director of the Society of the Propagation of the Faith. This essentially made Sheen, as a representative of the Sacred Congregation of the Propagation of the Faith in Rome, a missionary behind a desk—and a very powerful desk it became.

After his travels to missions of the world, Sheen was all the more enthusiastic to contribute to the evangelization of Africa, Asia and other continents. He was also eager to invite the people of the United States to join him in this mission.

The way Sheen saw it, the world suffered from "two kinds of hunger": the "hunger of the spirit" and the "hunger of bread."[20] He was determined to find a way to feed both of them. His solution was to inspire a mission mind among his fellow Americans. If the Western world helped satisfy the rest of the world's hunger for bread, they would simultaneously feed their own hunger of spirit. Sheen also felt that the personal call of all Christians was to obey the words of Christ to "go...and make disciples of all nations" (Matthew 28:19).

"Everyone in our office was a missionary," Sheen said, "those who opened the mail and typed, kept books, did the secretarial work, answered the mail....The good and faithful friends in our office are...sharers in the heavenly triumphs as much as those who left home for foreign missions."[21] His employees gave credit right back to Sheen. "You didn't work *for* him," Greg Hildebrandt explained. "You worked *with* him."[22]

Due to his visibility as a media star, the office was deluged with letters. Much of it was fan mail, but donations from average American citizens often accompanied the letters. Checks, sometimes cash—even coins taped onto letters—arrived by the truckload.

One Tuesday evening Sheen made an appeal to his television audience, asking each viewer to donate just one dime to the missions, and he was up to his knees in dimes by Friday afternoon. He soon learned that he had to be careful of what he said on television. On another occasion he mentioned his affinity for chocolate, and by the end of the week, he could barely walk down the hallway of his office because of all the boxes of chocolate cluttering his path.[23]

Thanks to the generosity of Americans—some of whom sacrificed vacation money and life savings—and to the many hands and hearts who worked together in the office in New York City, millions of dollars were sent to the missions all over the world. In the sixteen years Sheen served as director, the Society of the Propagation of the Faith raised close to two hundred million dollars, effectively quadrupling the average annual donations received by the office previously.[24] In a nutshell, Bishop Sheen was a fundraiser extraordinaire, but without his fellow "missionaries" in the office he never would have been able to keep track of it all.

INSPIRED BY SAINT PAUL

Sheen's missionary spirit was very much influenced and inspired by the model Saint Paul provided in the New Testament. In 1922, when Sheen was still a graduate student, award-winning French author Emile Bauman asked the rector of Louvain to recommend someone to accompany him on a journey retracing the steps of the great saint. Baumann was writing a book on Paul and wanted a companion who could assist him but also benefit from the pilgrimage. The rector suggested Sheen.

While retracing the steps of Saint Paul, Sheen reread the Acts of the Apostles and studied every letter of Paul in the Scriptures. The passage that made the deepest impression on Sheen was Paul's speech to the Athenians.

Paul did not talk down to the people of Athens, even though they were pagans and had evidence of their idolatry everywhere. While his Jewish spirit might have been repelled at the sight of the first commandment being so blatantly broken, Paul understood that the Greeks were gentiles—people of a different history, culture and background—and they needed to be approached with that understanding.

Sheen believed the saint's famous "Prayer to an Unknown God" discourse (see Acts 17) best displayed Paul's genius. In it he met the Greeks where they were. He first referenced a statue they had erected to an "unknown god," then told them that he knew the God that they did not and then explained who that God is.

However, the saint failed miserably to convert the Athenians, and Sheen wondered why. He came to the conclusion that it was because Paul failed to mention the *name* of Christ and to preach his crucifixion. Paul would later write in his Letter to the Corinthians that he decided "to know nothing among you except Jesus Christ and him crucified" (1 Corinthians 2:2). This would be the motto by which Paul would live the rest of his life. So perhaps he saw where he had made his mistake as well.

Even though Sheen was well aware that "preaching of the Word of God will always provoke antagonisms,"[25] his dream was to preach Christ and him crucified in Asia, particularly Japan and Communist China. In Japan he used Paul's famous address to inspire his own "unknown god" speech. Instead of a statue, however, Sheen used the iconic image of the shining sun on Japan's flag and their motto "The Land of the Rising Sun" as his talking points. He encouraged his Japanese listeners to reinterpret the symbol on the flag as Christ, changing "the Rising Sun" to "the Rising *Son.*"

The challenge of evangelizing China, Sheen thought, was not unlike the one Paul encountered in Greece. The Greeks had a very developed culture of art and philosophical thought. China too had a long and rich history and had evolved independent from the influences of other countries for thousands of years. Sheen believed this was all according to God's plan. He prophesied that one day China would become a great Christian nation.[26]

Also like the Greeks, China had its philosophers and sages. Sheen, who had read the wisdom of Confucius and familiarized himself with Buddhist philosophical thought, wrote in his autobiography, "Someday Buddha and Confucius may be to the Eastern Catholic theology what Plato and Aristotle were to St. Thomas and [St.] Augustine."[27]

Sheen grew to admire the contemplative spirit he found in the Far East, noting that while the West was ahead of the rest of the world when it came to taming the land, the East was far superior when it came to taming the self.

Sheen believed that evangelization needed to evolve. He thought that missionaries would do well to start with what was good about the religions they found in foreign countries. Once they found common ground for the foreign religion and Christianity, they could work their way up from there.

Christ himself modeled this sensitivity. He knew how to approach people slowly, starting with a common need. We see this in the Gospel of John, when Jesus asked the Samaritan woman at the well for a drink of water. By the end of that story, the Samaritan woman had left her bucket behind in her zeal to evangelize her fellow townspeople (see John 4:7–42).

While Sheen was on his world tour with Spellman, Chinese officials offered him an opportunity to further evangelize their country. They invited him to stay longer, tour the various Chinese universities and broadcast a series of talks. However, by this time the group was on the last leg of its tour, and the cardinal believed the United States needed Sheen more than China did.

Sheen was disappointed; the States were not. Sheen was poised to become the greatest missionary and convert-maker to ever walk on American soil.

"The Boss"

"MORALE AMONG [SHEEN'S] STAFF CAN CHALLENGE ANY in New York," wrote reporter James C.G. Conniff[1]—and it was no wonder, with their successful teamwork and the knowledge of all the good being accomplished urging them on. Most of the credit, Sheen felt, went to the practice of daily prayer. At 2:45 PM every workday, the staff in the national office stopped what they were working on and gathered for prayer. Sometimes they recited the rosary; other times they meditated on the Scriptures for fifteen minutes; often the bishop would give a brief talk on a religious theme.

After these prayer sessions Sheen would sometimes take a walk outside his office, located at 366 Fifth Avenue, in the heart of the city and very close to the Empire State

Building. Passersby often recognized him and greeted him with familiarity.

One day the bishop was walking by the former mansion of John Pierpont Morgan, which the Lutherans had purchased recently. A construction company had been hired to build a five-story building as an addition. One of the construction workers recognized Sheen and called out to him, "What do you think of us Catholics putting up a building for these lousy Methodists?"

Sheen corrected him: "They're not Methodists; they're Lutherans, and they are friends of ours."

One of the hardhats then looked up to a fellow worker, standing on a beam on the fifth floor, and bellowed, "All right, boys, put in the rivets!"[2]

Greg Hildebrandt sometimes accompanied "the Boss" (as everyone at the office referred to Sheen) during these walks. He noticed that anyone from a Park Avenue resident to a "street person" felt free to approach the bishop. Sheen would treat all with the same measure of friendliness and respect.

THE CHEERFUL GIVER

Hildebrandt also remembers that the bishop was always "extremely generous." As Sheen made his way down Thirty-Fourth Street, people would stop him and give him cash donations "for the poor." Then, perhaps ten minutes later, someone else would come up and ask for money. The bishop would respond by immediately handing over what he had just been given.[3]

Sheen didn't keep accounts or records of his finances, but there are countless stories that give witness to his generous spirit in action. He could be described as the kind of man who would give you the coat off his back. On a train ride once, Sheen did this literally. He encountered a fellow priest who lacked a proper coat and, moved at his plight, unhesitatingly handed over his new camel hair overcoat.[4]

Sheen also would give someone the clock off his mantelpiece or any object in his home if he saw that the person liked it. His giving was so automatic that if he was given a gift from a friend or admirer, that person often had to urge the bishop not to give it to someone else.

Sheen gave away money and clothes, found people work and helped set up hospitals. He even paid the orthodontist bills of a New York City garbage man's son after meeting the father on the street.[5] He was a tireless giver.

Wealthy patrons often named Sheen as a benefactor in their wills. Whenever he received these inheritances, he would immediately turn around and "invest" them in something like a school or a hospital. He also gave away most of the money he earned from his public speaking appearances and from the books he had published.

Whatever he didn't have to give he would help to raise. His fundraising skills allowed him to help the Sisters of Mercy open the Martin de Porres Maternity Hospital for black women in segregated Mobile, Alabama.[6]

For all the donations he received and for all the money he gave away, he was constantly deluged with mail asking for more. Employees, friends and family often questioned Sheen, feeling that he should be more discerning. How could he know that the person asking was actually disadvantaged and not taking advantage instead? Sheen's zeal for giving could not be diminished. He felt it was better to give than to take the chance of leaving someone in need.

"A Giving That Doesn't Measure"

While some thought it unwise of Sheen to fail to keep personal financial records, there were a number of reasons why he didn't. One reason was that he simply lacked the aptitude for that type of administration. While he was an exceedingly hard worker who could accomplish "ten times as much work as any businessman on Madison Avenue,"[7] the day-to-day details of pushing paper somewhat confounded the bishop. This is why he had his small army of thirty office assistants.

Sheen also felt that one of the dangers in the modern church was "the primacy of administration over love."[8] He would point out that in the book of Revelation, at the time of judgment, the bishops are condemned for a lack of spirituality, not for a lack of adequate bookkeeping.

Another reason Sheen didn't count his money was the same reason he told a young priest not to keep track of the number of converts he made. The priest told Sheen once, "I have already made seventy-two converts in six years of my priesthood." Sheen replied, "I would advise you to stop counting them, otherwise you might think you made them and not God."[9]

The money Sheen raised was for the poor, and to the poor was where it went—all for the glory of God. If he stopped to count what he had collected, he would be giving glory to himself. Seeing how much he had, he might even be tempted not to give it all away.

There were those who criticized the bishop for living in an expensive apartment in a tony neighborhood. His apparently posh lifestyle, many believed, was in direct contradiction to a priestly vow of poverty. (These people didn't realize that it is friars in religious orders and not diocesan priests who take that vow.)

According to Greg Hildebrandt, "People would say, look [where Sheen] lives…and he has a chauffeur…but these things were *nothing* in comparison to the millions he literally gave away.…People have *no* idea." Hildebrandt went on to say that Sheen was "passionate about the needs of the 'have-nots.'"[10]

The bishop saw his comfortable lifestyle as a way of life he could help others achieve. His desire was to elevate living conditions not just above the poverty line but ideally higher, at least to middle class, so that all people could have the chance to live happy, healthy, balanced lives. He hoped to empower people all over the world—not only by giving but also by inspiring them to be givers alongside him.

Sheen did not believe in romanticizing poverty. He believed that the Lord was born in poverty not because it was good to be poor but rather to inspire our charity. Poverty was something to rectify, not accept.

Wealth was not an automatic evil, nor was it a good in and of itself. It was good if it was used properly and an evil if it was idolized. Those to be admired and emulated were the poor who chose poverty, out of love for God and a detachment from things of the world, and the rich who, also detached from their worldly goods, were generous.

Wealthy Americans, Sheen felt, had special responsi-
bility to minister to the needs of the poor. He cited the fact
that this country, blessed as we are with material comfort,
was once a foreign mission itself. Sheen's great desire was to
increase the awareness of every Catholic American—no
matter what their financial circumstances were—to the
sufferings of their fellow men and to encourage them to
become more "mission-minded"[11] and recognize the ways
in which they could all help each other.

If only everyone could become a "fool for Christ" (see
1 Corinthians 4:10), Sheen once preached at a retreat, give
to others "without measure" and enjoy "the sheer ecstasy of
giving" with no "holding back." While perhaps not pleasing
to accountants, Sheen was certain the Lord approved of
this kind of foolishness.[12]

HUMANITY, HUMOR AND HOLINESS

In order to encourage the "mission mind" in American
teenagers, Fulton Sheen hired brothers Greg and Tim
Hildebrandt to work for the Society of the Propagation of
the Faith. "The boys," as Sheen would always refer to the
twins, were artists. The bishop had come across an impressive series of paintings they had done based on the passion
of the Christ. He admired their work, and upon learning
that the brothers were also filmmakers, he asked them to
come in for an interview.

The Hildebrandt brothers were both flattered and
intimidated to be summoned by such a famous and
respected personality. They wanted to make a good impression. They showed Sheen a documentary they had filmed

of the Sisters of St. Joseph in Kalamazoo, Michigan. They were surprised when Sheen began laughing not five minutes into the viewing. Apparently he found the narrative to be overly pious and unrealistic. He finally held up a hand between chuckles and said, "I've seen enough, boys!"[13]

Sheen was looking for realism, not Hollywood. He was looking for filmmakers to shoot the conditions of the countries where the missions were. They would later show the films in high schools across the United States to raise awareness among the nation's youth. The bishop gave the twins an assignment. "Boys, I want you to go shoot poverty in South America."[14]

When the brothers returned from their trip and showed the bishop their footage of the destitution they had found there, Sheen's reaction was entirely different from his response to the first film they had showed him. He was visibly moved, and afterward he pounded the table, exclaiming that something had to be done. He wished that he could send an army down to force South American governments to give the land and its wealth to the poor.

The bishop was known to speak out against governments, theories, philosophies—but not people. Both Robert Paul Mohan, a former student of the bishop, and actress Loretta Young, an admirer and friend, would say they never knew the bishop to criticize another person.[15]

Hildebrandt concurs. "The bishop was emotional; committed to God and humanity—he loved people." He was also "fantastically human." He had interests and hobbies and tastes like anyone else. Not a big fan of popular music, he nevertheless liked the Beatles when they first came out. In sports he admired Cassius Clay (later known as Muhammad Ali). Of the artists of the period, he was known to enjoy the surrealism of Salvador Dalí, while of Pablo Picasso he said, "That man believes nothing and therefore he paints nothing."[16]

Another interest of the bishop—perhaps due to his work in radio and television—was technology. He was always interested in seeing the latest developments in camera lenses and equipment, and he grew to enjoy computers immensely. He once announced to his office staff—in part astonishment and part amusement—that a computer had beaten him at another of his favorite pastimes, chess![17]

Sheen was famous for a "roaring laugh" that one could hear throughout the office. He was just as famous for making his employees roar. They all learned that the easy way to know where to find "the Boss" was to follow the sound of the laughter.

Working with the Society of the Propagation of the Faith launched the Hildebrandt brothers onto a career path that would make them famous in their own right. One fateful day in the mid-1960s, coworker Winnie Boyle saw Tim's sketch of an elfin figure.

"That looks like a Hobbit," she told him.

"What's that?" he asked, unfamiliar with the characters in the fantasy series created by Catholic J.R.R. Tolkien.[18]

A little over a decade later, the Brothers Hildebrandt, as they came to be called, would illustrate three calendars based on *The Lord of the Rings* trilogy. These sold in record-breaking numbers. They also painted the world-famous poster for the original *Star Wars* movie.

THE BISHOP AND WOMEN

It was women who really ran the office of the Society of the Propagation of the Faith during Sheen's tenure, and he was most appreciative of the help they were to him. As a small gesture of his gratitude, the bishop would invite all the women to join him for a tea and candy break in the afternoon.

Most of Sheen's female employees had worked with him for decades and were entirely devoted to the bishop for the rest of their lives. Obviously it wasn't the tea break that kept the women loyal to the priest. Nor was it his sense of humor. It was most likely the bishop had their support because he made it clear that "he had a huge respect and admiration for women," which distinguished itself from the more typical "pejorative mentality of [some] clerics of the time period."[19]

Always ahead of his time, Sheen believed that "women were coming into their own" in the church and that "the feminine principle in religion had been neglected." As a conciliar father at the Second Vatican Council, he regretted that his request for a document on women did not come to pass.[20] In his office Sheen was sure to entrust important responsibilities to his female employees, and he gave his full attention to their ideas and advice.

Sheen's high esteem for women and his love of the Blessed Mother were tied together. He explained this years later at a weekend retreat for priests. Sheen said that he had discovered that the level of any civilization could be measured by the level of its love for women.

He went on to explain that if someone loved music, for example, that person had to "go out to meet" it on its own terms and had to "obey its laws" in order to truly appreciate and enjoy music. A woman, Sheen said, must be approached and treated in much the same way. A man had to go out of himself to meet, appreciate and understand her. It therefore followed that the higher the "object of [his] love" was, the greater his love was called to be. The Virgin Mary, therefore, was deserving of the highest regard, and all women were deserving of respect.

Sheen resented the distortion of the quest for equal rights. He saw that "equality" between the sexes often was misunderstood to mean "interchangeability" between them. That was not what mutual respect and understanding between man and woman truly meant. Further, Sheen believed, this distortion was downright insulting to both genders. There was no shame in acknowledging that the genders were different from one another. Being different did not make equality with one another impossible. Men and women, after all, served one another in complementary roles.

Sheen felt that the argument for women in the priesthood was as pointless and uncharitable as men's complaint that women were given too important a role by God's coming to earth through Mary. "Why did God 'need' a woman?" they asked. "Couldn't he just appear without her 'help'?"

Jealousy and rivalry between the sexes was unchristian, Sheen believed. "There is no such thing as inferiority or superiority of one gender over another," he told a group of priests at one of his retreats. They were, however, different, which gave them different roles to play in God's plan.[21]

Edythe and Marlene Brownett were like the bishop's version of the biblical sisters Mary and Martha, who were close friends of Christ. Sheen knew the women from their girlhood, when their parents took them to watch live broadcasts of *The Catholic Hour*. From an early age the sisters listened to Sheen as he explained the Scriptures and church teachings. Sheen befriended the family and later offered the very attractive but "nun-like"[22] Edythe employment.

Edythe gave off something of a holy aura. A college graduate who had worked both in publishing and with foundling children before joining Sheen's office, she would go on to work for Sheen for the rest of his life. She had the important job of handling all private correspondence between Sheen and the Vatican. She also made his appointments and travel arrangements and performed all the other duties one expects from a personal assistant. Her familiarity with Sheen's life helped to cultivate in her a decided opinion about how he could best use his time and energy, and the bishop listened to her counsel.

Her sister Marlene went on to become a nun. Sister Marlene accompanied Sheen on his many trips to Fatima and was one of the few people allowed by his bedside when the bishop was hospitalized in his old age.

SEEING RED

As early as the 1930s, Sheen took an anti-Communist stance, becoming one of the most visible anti-Communist speakers in the country. The Communist Party had taken over Russia, China, Vietnam and Cuba. Priests and nuns who worked as missionaries in China were often arrested, imprisoned and tortured. They were then instructed to sign a confession that they were Communists and renounce their faith. Should they refuse, they suffered more torture. Many of them died.

One nun told Sheen that, when she was in a Communist prison, a guard handed her a lead pipe and instructed her to strike each of her fellow female inmates with it. Instead the nun gently touched the shoulder of each woman, as though knighting them. This infuriated the guard. "You're not a Communist!" he shouted. When the nun asked why not, he replied, "Because you don't hate."[23]

Russia had been an ally of the United States during World War II, so many Americans saw the country as a friend. Sheen too loved the country. It had been referred to previously as "Holy Mother Russia" for a reason. "Deeply embedded in the Russian soul were passionate religious convictions: the universal vocation…to call all men to brotherhood; the need of sacrifice and pain to accomplish this mission; and the supreme need of resigning oneself to God's will."[24]

Sheen recognized, however, that Americans could no longer call Russia a friend. Sheen sadly believed that the religious nature of Russians may have contributed to the country's becoming Communist in the first place. The Communist Party seemed to share and offer the same ideals as Christianity, only with a twist: "Brotherhood became revolutionary proletariat; sacrifice became violence, and the Will of God became the will of the dictator."[25]

Sheen's studies in philosophy had acquainted him with the works of Karl Marx, Vladimir Lenin and Joseph Stalin.

He believed that Communist philosophy could be summarized in three sentences: "Man has been 'alienated' from his true nature in two ways—by religion and by private property. Man was alienated from himself by religion, because it made him subservient to God; man was alienated from himself by private property because it made him subject to an employer. If, therefore, man was ever to be restored to his true nature, religion and private property must be destroyed."[26]

Like a mathematical equation or formula, this meant that Communism was therefore "inseparable" from atheism.[27]

As Sheen traveled the country speaking out against Communism, people who had escaped a Communist country often approached him with the offer to join his crusade or act as his informant. Whenever Sheen was suspicious of the person offering to "help" him, his first move was to call the FBI. His public position had earned him friends in the bureau, and he admired their work.

Sometimes the person was considered dangerous, and the bureau would instruct him to break contact. In other cases the FBI would place the person under surveillance. If the person was a trustworthy contact, the bureau would ask the bishop to keep communication open with him or her. One such informant told Sheen that at a Communist party meeting the bishop was referred to as "Public Enemy No. 1."[28]

Sheen eventually hired a bodyguard to accompany him on his speaking tours. The two had a routine. The guard would be introduced as a friend of Sheen and then sit by his side on the stage. As the bishop spoke, the bodyguard would scan the audience for known Communists. He would mark those he spotted with the letter "X" on a program and discreetly hand that program over to Sheen. This would give the bishop an idea of what he was up against.

On one particular night in Westchester, New York, Sheen glanced at the program and saw one giant "X." The entire audience seated in the lecture hall was Communist. Sheen had to think fast. He announced that since he had been accused of being unfair to Communists, he wished to rectify the situation. His lecture, therefore, would consist only of direct quotes from genuine Communist documents. So as not to be accused of misrepresenting the words, he asked that volunteers from the audience come forward to read those statements aloud from the stage.

No one volunteered. Sheen was able to finish the evening without disruption.

COMMUNIST CONVERSIONS

Communism was the subject of an episode of *Life Is Worth Living* one February night in 1953. In a truly inspired moment, the bishop read the burial scene from Shakespeare's *Julius Caesar*, replacing the names of the characters with those of Russian leaders. He spoke as if Stalin were at that moment in the throes of death. Ten days later Stalin actually *did* die. Many saw that evening's program as evidence of Sheen's prophetic powers. He was deluged with mail and phone calls. "How did you know?" everyone asked him.

To Sheen it was simply a coincidence. He knew, however, that the Lord could use his program in whatever way he saw fit, and Sheen was willing to be his instrument. One woman told the bishop that she had converted to the

Catholic faith because of that one episode. Her testimony made it all the clearer to Sheen that the credit belonged not to him but to God.

As the managing editor of the *Daily Worker,* Louis Budenz was a prominent New York City Communist who chose Christmas of 1936 to write a long article personally challenging Sheen on his public condemnation of Communism. Sheen published his reply in a pamphlet, which he made available to the general public for a nickel. Entitled *Communism Answers the Questions of a Communist,* it skillfully used Communist sources against themselves. Sheen followed up with a dinner invitation to Budenz to continue their dialogue.

Budenz, who had abandoned the Catholic faith in his youth, accepted the invitation, believing that he was more than up to the challenge. As both a labor leader and an attorney, he was a man used to winning. In the twenty-one labor disputes Budenz had argued in court, he had tasted victory all twenty-one times. However, Budenz would leave the dinner a changed man.

He was first stunned to find that Sheen was more well-versed in Communist history, documents and constitutions than he was. He was even more taken aback to find his soul "swept by love and reverence"[29] as never before.

In the following eight years Budenz often found himself reflecting on the events of that evening. Then he secretly approached Sheen about returning to the church. Sheen personally catechized Budenz, his wife and their three daughters in a series of classes in their home. He received the whole family into the church in October 1945.

When the news became public, the Communist Party in New York was humiliated. But Budenz's conversion didn't end there. After his baptism, he appeared at congressional hearings to speak out against Communism and would continue to do so until the end of his days. "Communism," Budenz ultimately learned, "is in unending conflict with religion and true freedom."

❧ 6 ❧

A Shepherd Looks for Sheep

THAT CONVERSION STORY HARDLY STANDS ALONE.
Everything the bishop did—his broadcasts, his writings, his
preaching from the pulpit—served two main purposes: one
was to bring souls to Christ, and the other was to give—
simply give—be it time, money or absolution. These two
goals, conversion and generosity, can be called the hall-
marks of Fulton Sheen's priesthood and life.

Sheen could only give what he himself had received.
The gift of faith had come in a mystical experience while he
was in the Seminary of St. Paul. He was at a conference
being conducted by his spiritual director, when the words
of the speaker seemed to fade away as a divine light illumi-
nated Sheen's mind. He felt bathed in spirit and enlight-
ened in mind. Within that moment he was completely sure

of the faith: in God, in his Son, in his Holy Spirit; in the faith of the Creed, the church and the pope.

Sheen never doubted his faith again. He knew this gift was not for him to keep to himself but to pass on to others. He did that with skillful and grateful alacrity for the rest of his life.

A PASSION FOR SOULS

Fulton Sheen could not shy from or be apologetic about his Catholic identity. Indeed, it would have been hard to be so while representing the church on national television. Extremely well-read, he was knowledgeable about the beliefs and tenets of other faiths, and he respected them, believing that Christ was "hidden in all world religions, though as yet His face is veiled."[1] He also felt that "the good Hindu, the good Buddhist, the good Confucianist, the good Moslem are all saved by Christ and not by Buddhism or Islam or Confucianism but through their sacraments, their prayers, their asceticism, their morality, their good life."[2]

These views, combined with his strength of faith, his breadth of knowledge and his persuasive way of speaking, enabled him to convert countless souls to Christ in his lifetime. He had an enormous amount of energy and "a deep passion for helping others find faith."[3] Some he would reach through his televised addresses. Others he was able to bring back to the fold through personal encounters and private instruction, despite his extremely busy schedule.

The bishop's converts ran the gamut from the homeless and forgotten to the leading intellectuals of the day, the wealthy and the famous. One person who embodied all three of the latter characteristics was Clare Boothe Luce.

An editor, a successful playwright and later a congress-woman and diplomat, Luce had mercilessly charged through her life, careers and marriages at full speed. This all came to a sudden halt when her nineteen-year-old daughter, Ann, died in a car accident. Mrs. Luce fell into a deep depression.

After a year of this, a concerned friend told the bishop about Luce's condition. Luce was not interested in religion, but she accepted an invitation to dine with the famous Fulton Sheen. With a "mind like a rapier,"[4] she was eager to engage in discussion with the eloquent and intelligent bishop.

When dinner was over, the bishop offered her an irresistible proposal: if she gave him five minutes to speak on God, he would give her an entire hour to argue her position. He had hardly started when she jumped out of her chair in disagreement. "If God is good, why did he take my daughter?"

The bishop replied with compassion, "In order that through your sorrow, you might be here now...to know Christ and His Church."[5]

Luce took instruction under Sheen for five months and was then received into the church. She never did anything halfway, and she embraced Catholicism with gusto. She became a great supporter and defender of the church, as well as a great friend to Sheen, for in him she had found not only a worthy teacher but a mind as brilliant as her own.

"DO NOT ASK ME TO GO TO CONFESSION."
Sheen was well aware of the important role the sacrament
of confession plays in changing lives. One winter he was
staying at St. Patrick's in the Soho area of London. A young
stage actress, who was appearing in a show across the street,
drunkenly stumbled into the church just as he opened the
front doors one bitter January morning. The bishop felt
moved to make her a cup of tea. After he had given her time
to warm up, he asked the unhappy woman to return later in
the day—perhaps before her matinee performance, when
she would be more rested and had sobered up.

The woman agreed to return, but only if he made a
promise not to ask her to go to confession. When he
assured her he would not, she asked him to repeat his
promise. He swore that he would not ask her to go to confession.

Later that afternoon the actress returned. As there
were art treasures in the church by such masters as Van
Dyck and Rembrandt, Sheen asked his guest if she would
like to see them. Walking down the aisle, the two passed by
the confessional, and before she could protest, the bishop
pushed the woman inside.

The bishop had kept his promise not to ask her to go to
confession. He proceeded to hear her confess. Two years
later she entered a convent, and Sheen had the happy honor
of presenting her with her veil.

Sheen's experience with converts and the miraculous
healing power of confession led him to reflect on their connection. In his book *Peace of Soul* he wrote:

The Church has a tremendous spiritual capital, gained through centuries of penance, persecution, and martyrdom; many of her children prayed, suffered, and merited more than they needed for their own individual salvation. The Church took these...merits and put them into the spiritual treasury, out of which repentant sinners can draw....This spiritual capital may be likened to a blood bank; whenever any of her members are suffering from spiritual anemia or the deep wounds of sin, the Church gives them a blood transfusion. She can never do it for us if we are spiritually dead in sin; a transfusion will not avail a corpse. So to obtain the indulgences or remission of the penalties of sin, the recipient must be in a state of grace, must have the intention of gaining the indulgences, and must perform the prescribed works.[6]

He explained further:

Every conversion starts with a crisis: with a moment or a situation involving some kind of suffering, physical, moral, or spiritual; with a dialectic, a tension, a pull, a duality, or a conflict. This crisis is accompanied, on the one hand, by a profound sense of one's own helplessness and, on the other hand, by an equally certain conviction that God alone can supply what the individual lacks.[7]

It is relatively unimportant whether the crisis...be sudden or gradual. What matters is struggle between the soul and God, with the all-powerful God never destroying human freedom. This is the greatest drama of existence.[8]

THE LOST ARE FOUND

This understanding prompted Sheen to keep an eye out for persons in crisis. He recognized how often their troubles were in truth the signs of the Shepherd's calling his lost sheep back to the fold.

Once while living in New York City, the bishop heard of a young man named Paul Scott who was a leper and needed help. The bishop had a special place in his heart for lepers. He had encountered them for the first time on a visit to the missions in Buluba, Uganda, and it had been a humbling experience.

Sheen had planned to pass out crucifixes to the 500 inhabitants of the leper colony. The first leper who came forward was missing half an arm, and he held out his other hand to receive the gift. Sheen inwardly recoiled at the sight of the "foul, noisome mass"[9] that was the leper's hand. Wishing to avoid actually touching the leper, he dangled the crucifix above the outstretched hand, then dropped it straight into the diseased area.

Suddenly the bishop saw the truth: while outwardly sick, the leper was far healthier on the inside than he was. Seized with shame and remorse, the bishop recovered the crucifix and presented it to the leper again, this time frater-nally pressing it into his hand. He went on to do the same for the 499 other lepers.

Sheen searched for six months for Paul Scott, and his determination paid off. He found a man whose hands and feet were painfully twisted and whose spirit was filled with bitterness and hatred. Paul's parents had thrown him out of their home when they discovered his disease.

Bishop Sheen instructed Paul in the faith. It took the man many months to work through his resentment, but eventually he was received into the church. He continued to visit the bishop as a weekly dinner guest, where, while preserving the young man's dignity, Sheen would cut his meat for him. The bishop also took it upon himself to find new living quarters for Paul and have them furnished for him as well.

Paul Scott was not the only New Yorker the bishop supported for years. Bishop Sheen did not just help a person once and then hope that he or she would go away. Nor did he bring them to the altar and abandon them once they had received their sacraments. He had a great love for people and a true concern for their spiritual and physical welfare. He invested a lot of time and interest in each particular case he became involved in, and apparently the more challenging the individual in need, the more Fulton Sheen liked him or her.

One Good Friday afternoon, after preaching on the Crucifixion, a troubled and disheveled woman accosted Sheen and cursed him viciously. After he managed to calm her, she revealed that his meditation on the good thief had struck her heart. She had come into the church intending to steal purses but hadn't, upon hearing his words. The woman also confessed her past to him. She had left the church as a teenager, she confided. She was wanted by the FBI.

The bishop persuaded the woman to receive the sacrament of penance. She did and began receiving Communion daily. Charges against her eventually were dropped, and since she was in no condition to work, the bishop arranged for her financial support for the remaining twenty years of her life.

Another woman, Kitty, was a twenty-one-year-old streetwalker lying close to death after her husband had poisoned her. She lived in the dirtiest slum the bishop had ever seen. Kitty proclaimed to Sheen that she was "the worst girl in the city of New York."

The bishop corrected her. "You are not…; the worst girl in the city of New York says that she is the best girl in the city of New York."[10]

Sheen did not believe pride was among this girl's many sins. After a half hour of begging to hear her confession, the bishop was able to absolve young Kitty right before she began to hallucinate. She was taking a turn for the worse, slipping in and out of consciousness, so the bishop quickly administered the sacrament of the sick.

Kitty immediately began to recover. Renewed and strengthened, she resolved to prove she could be good. She became Kitty the Apostle. Working with the bishop to save souls, she encouraged all those she encountered on the street to go to confession and change their lives as she had. For the remaining years Bishop Sheen served at St. Patrick's, he would hear confessions that began, "Kitty sent me."

"WE ARE ALL SINNERS"

Sheen's knowledge of his own sinfulness was of great help to him when he visited prisons. Whenever he began to preach at a prison retreat, he set the tone right away by announcing, "Gentlemen, there is one great difference between you and me. You have been caught; I was not. In other words, we are all sinners."[11]

While they were not required to attend his retreats, 95 percent of the prisoners in one jail attended—some rushing to claim seats an hour early. Once they discovered that Sheen would stop and speak with those seated along the aisle, those became the most coveted seats in the house.

Sheen treated the prisoners as he did everyone: with respect and compassion. He addressed them as "gentlemen"; he touched them, laughed with them and made every effort to show them that they were all on the same level.

The prisoners were grateful for the manner with which he expressed his love and acceptance of them; for many it was the first time they were treated with such regard. They felt valued, and they expressed their love in their letters and cards to the bishop after his visits.

At the end of one visit, an entourage of prisoners walked Sheen to the front gates as a send-off. Sheen felt his zucchetto in his pocket, and instead of putting it on, he turned to the inmate nearest him and gave it to him as a gift. The prisoner was stunned. "Is this for me?" he asked, and he began to cry.

Two months later Sheen received a package from the prison. He tore it open to find a painting of the crossbars of a cell with a pair of hands stretching out from them. In their calloused palms lay a purple zucchetto.[12]

The idea of man's sinfulness is a stumbling block to many. If they cannot admit that they sin, they can neither reap the benefits of the sacrament of confession nor humble themselves to receive the salvation of the cross.

One time back when the bishop was teaching at the university, he had an interesting conversation with Madame Koo, the wife of a Chinese ambassador. She claimed that the doctrine of original sin was the most stupid religious tenet she had ever heard, which was why she was a Buddhist. The bishop asked her to explain the doctrine of the eightfold path to him, even though he was already familiar with it. Once she did, he challenged her: How could man be perfect if Buddha himself instructed that there was a need for purification?

Madame Koo experienced a new kind of enlightenment that day. Later she would leave the path of Buddha to walk the way of Jesus Christ and his church.[13]

ABRAHAM'S CHILDREN

Bishop Sheen felt a tender love toward his Jewish brothers and sisters, for he appreciated the Catholic roots found there. He believed, "For a Catholic, to be anti-Semitic is to be un-Catholic."[14] "Christianity," he wrote, "honors Abraham, Isaac, Jacob, Moses, David. Were not the twelve Apostles Jews? Was not the first Pope a Jew? Does not the Church use the Old Testament as much as the Synagogue does?"[15]

The bishop enjoyed some extraordinary encounters with Jews during his lifetime, and he would never fail to freely extend the love of Christ to them.

A young Jewish boy from Pittsburgh was told he was too young to wear a yarmulke. He had seen the bishop wearing his zucchetto on television, and believing it was a yarmulke, he secretly wrote to the bishop to ask if he could

have it. Sheen mailed it off to him, and the boy was pic-
tured in local newspapers wearing it proudly.

Many years later in New York, a kind Jewish man called
one day from his jewelry shop and asked if Sheen would
like a bag of silver crucifixes. The bishop went down to look
at them and asked the jeweler, his friend of twenty-five
years, where they had come from.

The jeweler said in disgusted disbelief, "From Sisters."
He had been shocked when they told him that they felt
wearing the crucifixes "separated" them from the world.
They then asked the jeweler how much he would give them
in exchange for them.

"I weighed them out thirty pieces of silver," he said.
Shaking his head, he asked the bishop, "What is wrong with
your Church?"

The bishop answered, "Just that! The contempt of
Christ and His Cross which makes it worldly!"

This encounter was a turning point in Sheen's relationship with the jeweler, who would die a Christian.[16]

Even while bedridden in the last years of his life, the
bishop was indefatigable about bringing souls to Christ.
When he was in the hospital recovering from heart surgery,
a Jewish gentleman visited the bishop every day for several
months. Then he didn't come for a number of days. When
he finally returned, he explained that his wife was sick. She
was undergoing treatment for cancer; the doctors would be
operating the next day.

Bishop Sheen handed the man a small silver crucifix
that had been blessed by Pope John XXIII. He said with all
confidence and gentleness that, as it depicted Christ's

death on a cross, it was Jewish, and because of this, "I know you will revere it." He went on, "I will only tell you that He was Jewish on His Mother's side. Who was His Father, you will have to find out.... But if you throw your trust with the well-being of your wife into His hands, you may one day discover who His Father is."

Some days later the gentleman returned to report that his wife would not need surgery. Exposing the crucifix he now wore around his neck, he told the bishop, "I found out Who Christ's Father was."[17]

"Not...until the Jew defends the Christian and the Christian the Jew," Sheen once prophesied, "will there be peace."[18]

ISLAM

Sheen did not have many encounters with Muslims. He finally met some while on a mission tour of Africa.

Islam rejects Christ as God-made-man and upholds Muhammad as the ultimate prophet. Sheen felt that the history of Islam's antagonism toward Christianity came from a misinterpretation of the Christian belief in the Holy Trinity. Muslims saw this belief as polytheistic (believing in many gods).

Muslims believe in the absolute sovereignty of one God. For this, and for their faithfulness to prayer, Sheen believed they deserved some credit. He noticed the Muslim fidelity to prayer in his encounters in Africa. Followers of Islam are required to pray five times a day, and Sheen often saw a Muslim stop what he was doing, take out a prayer rug and bow down to God.

Sheen also noted that the Blessed Mother had a place of honor in the Koran, the book of Islam. On the death of his daughter Fatima, Muhammad stated that she was in paradise and was second in holiness only to the Virgin Mary. Sheen thought it was interesting that while he elevated his daughter, Muhammad held the belief that Mary's sanctity was superior to that of all other women.

Sheen noticed another connection between Mary and Muhammad's daughter. The Blessed Mother began to appear to three young children in the small town of Fatima, Portugal, in 1917, calling for prayer and peace. Portugal had been conquered by the Muslims, who then occupied the country for centuries. They in turn were driven out by the Catholics about one hundred years before the visions took place. Sheen wondered if there was any connection between the revelations of Our Lady of Fatima, as she came to be called, and what he hoped would be the ultimate conversion of the Muslims.[19]

Sheen was very interested in interreligious dialogue and became well-known for ecumenical efforts, which would only increase through the years. He was, of course, completely orthodox in his teachings and his practice of the Catholic faith, often being recognized by the Vatican for this. However, he had an enviable way of reaching non-believers.

Sheen described this ability to stand up and explain his faith while accepting and embracing those of other faiths as an attitude all Catholics should have. He believed that while Catholics "should be intolerant of false doctrine," their attitude "toward those who hold it" should be nonjudgmental.[20]

He added, "We should realize that all religions...have a small or large arc of the circle of truth....Each expresses one or another of the yearnings of the human race toward the infinite; each sounds at least one true note on the keyboard of Divine religion."[21]

Sheen went on to encourage peace by publicly stating, "Historical clashes between Moslemism and Christianity in the past must not impede reconciliation and affection among peoples."[22]

The United States was involved in the Cold War in those days, and Communism and its threat of global domination—or destruction—became a major concern of the average American citizen. Islam and its ancient history as a conquering world power was not apparent to the American consciousness. All the while it quietly thrived under the radar, growing into the world's most practiced religion. Sheen was one of the few Americans who noticed, and as early as 1952, he prophesied that, for better or for worse, Muslims may "hold the key to world order."[23]

HUMBLE GRATITUDE

While Sheen may have been "proud" of the great number of converts he helped, he refused to take credit for them. He freely admitted that he could no more make a person a Christian "by my influence than I could turn a sawdust doll into a pretty child of six."[24]

Too often the word *conversion* is taken to mean a change in who a person is, when it in fact means a complete change in the direction the person is headed. The bishop encountered many travelers who were off course and lost, and he helped them to get back on the road. To some he would give directions, to others a map; still others he might accompany on the way. In the end it was up to each individual traveler to decide the destination, get there and all the more remain there.

Knowing this, Bishop Sheen experienced a profound gratitude at being allowed to act as an instrument of God's grace. One day he received a special confirmation that he was doing the work to which God had called him and that he should continue doing it.

He was on a pilgrimage to the Holy Land. At four o'clock one morning in Galilee, he sat down by the shore of the Sea of Tiberias in order to reflect on the Scripture passage found in the twenty-first chapter of the book of John.

The old expression "by hook or by crook" had always amused Sheen because it was so easy to apply to the spiritual life. Jesus often compared himself to a fisherman catching men instead of fish—using a "hook"—or to a shepherd tending a flock of lambs—using a "crook." However, these comparisons confused Sheen in this particular story in John's Gospel.

He read that seven apostles had gone out together for an early morning fishing excursion. He looked out to sea and noticed something "coincidental": He saw seven men out on a boat too. Meanwhile, in the story the resurrected Jesus is on the shore. He builds a fire and cooks breakfast for his apostles. After they return and eat, Jesus takes Peter aside. He tells Peter, who is a fisherman by trade, to *feed his sheep.*

Sheen was stumped. The leap from fish to sheep failed to make sense to him. Jesus usually used the immediate environment to make his analogies. Why speak of lambs that grazed in the fields when walking by the sea? Yet the Lord had told Peter this three times in a row, using the two words *sheep* and *lambs*. Finally Sheen gave up trying to figure it out.

At that moment there was a tap on his shoulder, and Sheen turned around. A man stood before him holding a three-day-old lamb, which he gently placed in the stunned Sheen's arms.

"Where did you find this lamb?" Sheen asked, astonished.

"I am a shepherd," the man answered. "I graze my flock on this field adjoining the Sea of Tiberias."[25]

So the fish of the sea and the sheep of the field were not separate after all. Flocks could be found just past the rocky outcropping where Sheen sat. Sheep probably frolicked within the line of vision of Jesus and his apostles that day as well. It all made sense now.

As he cradled the precious lamb to himself, Sheen felt unworthy of being entrusted with the innocent bundle and of having received the answer to his question in such a beautiful fashion. He must have felt humbled too when recalling the specifics of that Bible passage:

The Lord asked Peter, "Son of John, do you love me?"

"Yes, Lord; you know that I love you," Peter replied.

"Feed my lambs," Jesus instructed.

Sheen had been christened Peter, and his father was named John. God had called him to be a shepherd—complete with his "crook" or *crosier*. The command was to Sheen, as successor to the apostles, just as much as it had been to Saint Peter, leader of the original twelve.

Sheen had his photograph taken with the lamb as he stood by the Sea of Tiberias. It would become his favorite portrait, serving as a humbling reminder that the best way to express his love for the Lord was by feeding his sheep.

❊ 7 ❊

Brothers in the Lord

GIVEN SHEEN'S POSITION AS THE MOST INFLUENTIAL cleric in the United States, it is no surprise that he built lasting relationships with several members of the hierarchy, including five popes. Most of these relationships were mutually supportive. In the highly public one that wasn't, Sheen managed to function as a kind and forgiving brother, despite his pain.

CLASHES WITH THE CARDINAL

Sheen and Cardinal Francis Spellman share a legendary reputation as "battling bishops." Thomas C. Reeves, in his book *America's Bishop,* traced the trouble to an original dispute between the two. There were actually two incidents, very similar in nature. In each episode Spellman requested money from the Society of the Propagation of the Faith while Sheen was heading it, and Sheen turned him down. Spellman interpreted Sheen's rejections as disobedience from a man he saw as something of a protégé.

The first major clash happened in 1955. Spellman asked that funds raised and collected through the Society of the Propagation of the Faith be used to accelerate the distribution of food to war-torn Europe. Sheen did not document his reasons for refusing this request, but they were apparently economic. The United States government was already providing foodstuffs for Europe, and the expenses for their delivery were divided between the United States and the countries receiving the aid. There seemed little reason to begin paying for services that others were providing already, even if it was to "help speed things up." The society's financial resources were limited, and their allocation had to be wisely determined.

Cardinal Spellman was not used to being refused. Through correspondence, face-to-face meetings and influential mutual acquaintances, he tried to persuade Sheen to see his side. One of his arguments was that he wanted those receiving the aid to know that the food distribution program was of Catholic origin. He saw it as an evangelization tool, fearing that Protestant relief services would send food and thereby win influence. The program provided relief to peoples of all faiths.

Sheen did not see competing with Protestants for proselytizing rights as a primary concern. He hardly saw how a desire to show up Protestants could be a legitimate motive to hand over funds.

Spellman and Sheen were both stubborn. The more

Spellman pressured Sheen to see his side, the more Sheen dug in his heels. They seemed to speak different languages. Spellman was stunned by Sheen's immovability and saw it as "the first direct act of non-compliance with a suggestion that I have made...during the seventeen years I have been privileged to be the Archbishop."[1] He interpreted Sheen's "no" as a personal insult.

Determined to resolve the situation to his satisfaction, Spellman took action. He appealed to wealthy patrons like Joseph Kennedy, to the general council of the Society (who took Sheen's side) and finally to the pope. After some months the situation was finally examined. Spellman received word from the Vatican: the pope had denied his request for funds. Spellman had lost the battle.

Spellman had not lost his fighting spirit, however. Less than two years later he again requested money from Sheen and the Society, this time demanding payment in the millions for powdered milk and other surplus goods he had supplied to the Society to distribute to the poor. Sheen refused on the grounds that the surplus goods had been freely donated to Spellman and the church by the federal government. If they hadn't cost Spellman a penny, why should he be reimbursed?

It was Sheen who appealed to Rome this time for support. The pope was ill, so he deferred from meeting with them for some months. Finally he decided again in Sheen's favor.

SILENCE IS GOLDEN

Bishop Sheen rarely mentioned his clashes with Spellman to others. He was a private man, and he found the conflicts a great source of suffering. When he did allude to the incidents, he tended to do so in a general manner and with humorous undertones, as he enjoyed entertaining others with stories. He believed that silence was often the best recourse, in order to avoid the temptation of self-justification.

Through God's grace Sheen was able to channel his sufferings and put them to good use. It was during this period that he wrote *Life of Christ.* What better way to deal with his trials than to bring them to the cross and meditate on the one who was crucified?

Later, when writing his autobiography, Sheen was well aware that people were interested in having him expose the cardinal in some way. Instead he reminded his readers of David's reply when asked why he was allowing himself to be stoned by a member of Saul's family: "If the Lord has told him to curse David, who can question it?" (see 2 Samuel 16: 5–13). Sheen added that he was "certain that it was God Who made certain people throw stones at me, but I am just as certain that I have thrown stones at other people, and for those stonings I beg mercy and pardon."[2]

Sheen saw spiritual stonings as part of the purification process. He once compared this process to that of a piece of marble's being slowly transformed into a work of art at the hand of the Master Sculptor, God himself: "A sculptor who wishes to carve a figure out of a block uses his chisel, first cutting away great chunks of marble, then smaller pieces, until he finally reaches a point where only a brush of hand is needed to reveal a figure. In the same way, the soul has to undergo tremendous mortifications at first, and then more refined detachments, until finally its Divine image is revealed."[3]

Having a kind word for everyone was a trait Sheen had inherited from his mother. When Cardinal Spellman died of a stroke in 1967, Bishop Sheen proved that he truly believed in peace, forgiveness and brotherhood when he wrote, "In life, [Spellman] claimed our attention, our respect and our love. That does not deny him in death the even more beautiful tribute of our prayers."4

THE VICAR OF CHRIST

The pope was the Antichrist, claimed a Pennsylvania man. This man had twelve books to prove it, and he was all set to send them to the bishop. Then he heard Sheen speak about the Holy Father on television.

The man wrote to Sheen, "I was waiting for you to talk about the Pope but what you said about the Holy Father and the Vicar of Christ, I rather liked."5

Fulton Sheen was a great defender of the papacy. He trusted in the authority of the pope and pledged to stay faithful to the Vicar of Christ for as long as he lived. He once stated, "Attacks against the Church have hurt me as much as attacks against my own mother."6

Sheen defended the pope so passionately because he had read in the Scriptures of how Jesus had prayed in a special way for Peter to lead the others properly, especially through difficult times. Sheen explained:

> Though the other Apostles were there, [Our Blessed Lord] spoke only to Peter: "Peter, I have prayed for you." Our Lord did not say: "I will pray for *all* of you." He prayed for *Peter* that his faith fail not, and after he recovered from his fall that he confirm his brethren. I think

bishops are strong *only* when they are united with the
Holy Father. As we begin to separate from him, we are
no longer under the prayer of Christ. And…we are no
longer protected, nor are we strong guardians or angels
of the churches.[7]

A young fan, on the occasion of the bishop's eighty-fourth
birthday, expressed his desire to see Sheen seated on the
Chair of Peter: "I hop you have a happy birthday.…And I
hop that one day you will be Pop."[8]

Sheen had no papal aspirations. He was honored whenever he received an invitation from the Vatican to a private
audience with the pope. He had his first, with Pope Pius
XI, while he was still a student at Louvain.

The pope had been a librarian and was a very learned
man. Upon hearing that Sheen was a student at Louvain, he
tested his knowledge with questions. Sheen was embarrassed
when the pope asked him if he had ever read the works of
Aloysius Taparelli and he had to answer "no." The pope took
him by the hand and asked him to promise to buy two vol-
umes by the Italian Jesuit philosopher the moment he left
the Vatican and to "read every line."[9] Sheen immediately
purchased two books and read every Latin syllable.

Pope Pius XII was not yet pope when Sheen met him
for the first time. He was Cardinal Eugenio Pacelli, the
Secretary of State at the Vatican. Sheen recalled that the
two conversed in Pacelli's office for over an hour, con-
demning the evils of Nazism.

Pacelli believed that since Catholicism had evolved
from Judaism, Catholic Christians shared in the lot of the

Jews in many ways. As pope he would forge strong ties with Jewish leaders and even come to their aid against the Nazis. Eugenio Zolli, the highest ranking rabbi in Rome during the Second World War, would later convert to the Catholic church, noting, "You could say of the reign of Pius XII that it was inspired by the words of the prophet Isaiah: 'Peace is harmony, peace is salvation for those who are near as for those who are far, I wish to heal all'" (see Isaiah 57:19).[10]

Pius XII took on the theme of peace for his papacy. He would consecrate Sheen a bishop in Rome, and in private he was known to have such a high regard for Sheen that he called him by his first name.[11]

One time Pius XII conveyed this esteem in a way that astonished Sheen. The pontiff, expecting Sheen for a private audience, prepared a statement to present to him. The two were engaged in a discussion about the topics Sheen wished to cover on the upcoming episodes of *The Catholic Hour* when the pope suddenly stood up from his desk. Sheen followed suit, jumping up from his chair, although he did not know what was going on. The pope then picked up the piece of paper on which he had composed his statement and began reading off a litany of praise about Sheen's gifts of prophecy. Sheen was humbled and consoled by the pope's supportive demonstration.[12]

GOOD POPE JOHN

The next pope also became a real friend to Sheen. The jolly and simple son of a sharecropper, Pope John XXIII would shatter the image of the pope as a pious and remote figure. He was a large man, earthy and robust. He looked people in the eye, slapped them on the back, cracked jokes and treated everyone like family. His new "people's pope" approach was a style that would make him beloved.

John XXIII had been born Angelo Roncalli, and like Sheen he came from a farming family where money was hard to come by. This background had made him ideal to take on the position of president of the Italian Office of the Propagation of the Faith, to which he had been appointed in 1921.

He and Sheen had more in common than their work for that office and their love for the missions. They were both known to be humble, and both had a sense of humor. The two men seemed to recognize the holiness in the other.

Sheen immediately liked the down-to-earth pontiff upon meeting him, and he always trusted his first impressions. Sheen was one to appreciate straightforwardness. He admired the pope's utter lack of pretension.[13]

He also appreciated the pope's sense of humor. The pope was known to make fun of himself. He is quoted as saying, "Anybody can be Pope; the proof of this is that I have become one," and, "It often happens that I wake up at night and begin to think about a serious problem and decide I must tell the Pope about it. Then I wake up completely and remember that I am the Pope."[14]

Whenever Sheen visited the Vatican, the pontiff went out of his way to be gracious to him. He presented Sheen with gifts and posed for photographs with him, saying, "It may make some in the Church jealous, but that will be fun."[15] Informed of the struggles Sheen had undergone with Spellman, the pope acknowledged, "You have suffered much.... [Your sufferings] will bring you to a high place in Heaven."[16]

Another time John XXIII invited Sheen to his hometown in the province of Bergamo to visit his family. When Sheen arrived, the whole town showed up to welcome him, displaying the same level of hospitality for which the pope was known.

Many people expected the papacy of the cheerful farmer pope to be quiet and short-lived. While his reign *was* brief, it was also one of the most pivotal in the history of the church. In less than five years he would prove to be a powerful and confident leader who would be responsible for bringing the church more fully into the twentieth century.

VATICAN II

The pope chose Christmas Day 1961 to announce to the world that he would be calling for a Second Vatican Council.[17] After much preparation, the council officially opened on October 11, 1962. Some twenty-six hundred bishops were present. For Fulton Sheen, the experience of being an active part of church history would be an honor he would treasure as a great blessing.[18]

Representatives from all over the world were in attendance, and the proceedings were convened in Latin. Council sessions were held from 9:00 AM to 12:30 PM every weekday, and priests said Mass every day. One of Sheen's favorite daily events was hearing the priests sing the Creed together. It was almost miraculous to see men from countries that were clashing politically or even militarily in the outside world unite in harmonious song and profess their shared faith under the dome of St. Peter's. Sheen felt that the cooperative spirit he experienced at the council "would make the United Nations blush for want of a common commitment."[19]

Fittingly, the first proclamation the council officially announced to the world was the message that all men were brothers regardless of race or nationality. It was therefore very irritating to the bishop to discover that the media chose to focus on the disagreements the bishops were having with one another. Bishop Sheen scolded the reporters. Of course there would be disagreements; the whole point of the council was to discuss, debate, define, defend and eventually decide together.

Sheen told the journalists to research the first council of the church, which was held in Jerusalem, as recorded in the book of Acts (15:1–29). This would help them recognize that disputes were normal to the process. However, in the end Sheen saw that a journalist could not understand how a church council worked if he or she did not carry the Spirit of Christ within.[20]

Two great tiers of seats were set up in the nave of the basilica. They were ten rows high and 360 feet long, stretching from the inner doors to the tomb of Saint Peter.[21] Underneath these were two coffee bars. The bishops cleverly dubbed one "Bar-Jona" or "Son of John," which was the "surname" of Saint Peter. Congregating around the coffee bar created great camaraderie among the bishops. They would joke and tease one another in a brotherly fashion.

Sheen wrote in his autobiography, "One aspect of the Council that has been rarely touched upon is the humer....When one expects another life than this one,...then there is no burden to take the world too seriously."[22] In keeping with this idea, Bishop John P. O'Loughlin of Australia composed a limerick at the beginning of the council:

> Call us comrades or cobblers or mates,
> Or even buddies, the term in the States.
>   Secure in the knowledge
>   We belong to the College
> With the Pope we're to have tête-à-têtes.

Bishop O'Loughlin and the other bishops would continue to produce such poems as a humorous record of events for the remainder of the council.[23]

It would take three years, divided into four sessions, to cover all thirteen subjects to be addressed. A bishop was allowed to express his views on any subject by written submission or by presenting an oral "intervention" in Latin. Speakers were limited to ten-minute orations. If they exceeded their limit, a bell would ring and the person would be asked to sit down—even if he was a cardinal, Fulton once noted in a letter to a friend.

Sheen found the most riveting talks came from bishops who had truly suffered for the faith. He was startled but inspired by the appearance of the Yugoslavian bishop, who was disfigured as the result of being doused with gasoline and set on fire by Communist oppressors.

Pope John XXIII died of stomach cancer on June 3, 1963. Sheen was sorry to lose a man he had not only held in high esteem, due to both his office and character, but also considered a friend. Pope Paul VI was elected pope, and the council resumed on September 29, 1963.

"SHEEN WILL SPEAK"

Early in the proceedings Sheen had been named to the Conciliar Commission on the Missions. It was a comfortable fit. The bishop truly considered himself a missionary after his many years with the Society of the Propagation of the Faith. After all, 70 percent of the donations collected for the society worldwide came from the United States,[24] thanks to Sheen's ability to inspire the American people to give.

So it was that on November 9, 1964, Sheen was called on to address his fellow bishops at the council. Cardinal Agagianian had been speaking but was cut short by Cardinal Felice, who told him, "Sheen will speak."[25] Sheen then got up as the last speaker on the subject of the missions. Word quickly spread that he was to give his intervention, and the coffee bars emptied as everyone returned to their seats.

Sheen's talk focused on the spirit of poverty. He proclaimed, "As chastity was the fruit of the Council of Trent, and obedience the fruit of the First Vatican Council, so may the spirit of poverty be the fruit of this Second Vatican Council."[26]

Sheen said the missions were to be found not in territories but in souls. If the church focused on people, then she would find her missions. Wherever poverty was to be found, Sheen said, wherever people were burdened by material needs and spiritual wants, wherever there was a lack of priests to serve, that was where the missions were.

He pushed for more efforts to address the poverty in Africa, South America and Asia. He spoke with passion and conviction as he continued, "As only a wounded Christ can convert a doubting Thomas, so only a Church wounded by poverty can convert a doubting world."[27]

Not only did Sheen speak longer than any American at the council, but he went over the time limit. Interestingly, Sheen did not hear the dreaded *Habe excusatum, Pater, sed tempus jam elapsum est,* "Excuse me, Father, but your time is up."[28] He didn't hear the bell either. All interventions were submitted to Cardinal Felice ahead of time for approval. Apparently, what he had to say was considered important enough to bend the rules. Applause followed his speech.

Sheen was very involved in the prayerful, painstaking care that went into creating each of the four constitutions, nine decrees and three declarations that were promulgated during that historic time. He prophesied, "It will be a different world at the end of the Council,"[29] and he was right. Pope John XXIII had summoned Vatican II for what he called the *aggiornamento* or renewal of the church. Renewal came. Many Catholics felt it was the breath of fresh air the church needed. Others feared what the changes might mean to the church.

The council ended on December 8, 1965, the Feast of the Immaculate Conception. It was fitting that something first announced on Christmas Day four years previous was completed in the Advent season. Bishop O'Loughlin observed this in the last limerick he would write on the council:

As we bishops depart from old Roma
We can proudly display our diploma
At the Council's finale
We say "buon natale"
And "goodbye" to Bar-Jona's aroma.[30]

THE CHURCH OF ROCK AND WATER

Sheen returned home with renewed enthusiasm, looking forward to participating as best he could in a reawakened and more vibrant church. He strongly believed that the Second Vatican Council was an idea whose time had come. For example, before the council he had wanted to celebrate Mass in the vernacular,[31] as he was eager to help people grasp the meaning behind the beautiful words of the Consecration.

The council decisions, made in the Spirit, were neither conservative nor liberal. Sheen thought these terms were used to further a political agenda rather than to further God's spiritual one. For the church to be truly healthy and in balance, it must be the solid foundation of rock from which living waters flow. He explained:

> In Scripture the Church is symbolized as the rock that was struck and from which came living waters. The rock is permanent, the waters represent the change and dynamism of the Church. The psychotics hold to the rock and forget the waters; the neurotics swim in the waters and forget the rock.... The psychotics would isolate the Church from the world; the neurotics would identify the Church with the world. For the psychotics religion is cultic; for the neurotics it is activistic.[32]

Sheen's example from the Scripture is a call to the church to recover from the surprise of our woundedness and believe in the life-giving and cleansing properties of the water, without succumbing to "grumbling in the desert" as the Israelites did. Only then will Vatican II succeed in carrying out God's will for people and the church.

Less than a year after the end of the Second Vatican Council, Bishop Sheen was summoned to Rome. There the pope informed him that he would be transferred from the archdiocese of New York.

This must have come as a surprise to Sheen. He was immensely popular in his adopted city, as well as in Rome, for his incredibly successful work in collecting money for the Society of the Propagation of the Faith. Suddenly he was to leave his post at the Society and New York City altogether, to take on a totally new kind of assignment.

At seventy-one years old, Sheen was also at an awkward age to be changing jobs. Ever the obedient one, however, Sheen accepted his "marching orders" and prayerfully looked over the list of potential dioceses from which Rome asked him to choose.

Years before Sheen had fished a crumpled sheet of paper out of the pope's wastepaper basket in order to preserve the words *Nolo sine cruce crucifixum,* "I don't wish to be crucified without a cross." Now Sheen was standing in the papal offices once again, looking over another piece of paper. The diocese of Rochester was on the list. It was a troubled town, suffering from recent race riots and crippling inner-city poverty. It was in the state of New York, which may be why Sheen chose it to be his own. In doing so, he perhaps unknowingly accepted the cross on which he would be crucified.

Banished?

"GUESS WHO OUR NEW BISHOP IS!"

Brother Andrew Apostoli paused in the middle of drinking a cup of coffee and looked up at the fellow Franciscan who had just burst into the kitchen. "Who?"

"Fulton Sheen!"

Apostoli put his cup down. "Oh, come on…!" This brother must be joking, he thought. Sheen was too big, too famous. How could he be the new archbishop of little old Rochester?[1]

Many people shared Apostoli's reaction to Sheen's appointment. Some even felt that it was an insult to the bishop, a form of exile. They believed that having him sent off to a "microscopic diocese"[2] would signal the end of his religious career.

Others felt that presiding over his own diocese would be an honor for the bishop, one he had awaited for a long time. While the setting was not ideal or glamorous, Sheen certainly deserved the "promotion." And the people of Rochester could be grateful to have such an esteemed figure as their bishop.

Sheen, in his autobiography, never once questioned or complained about his fate. He spoke of his experiences as bishop of Rochester in only appreciative and positive tones. The only negative comments he would record covered the failings he found in himself while there. He would, in fact, suffer much in Rochester, undergoing a spiritual desolation comparable to a dark night.

A WARM RECEPTION

The passion of Jesus began on a high note: cheering crowds greeted him when he entered Jerusalem. Sheen's spiritual passion began in much the same way. A cheering crowd of three thousand people gathered at the airport to welcome him to Rochester on the Feast of Saint John of the Cross, December 14, 1966. He received the goodwill of the people with his usual gratitude, grace and charm. He joked, "Now you've seen me live, and I'm sure you are disappointed."[3]

He then paid the diocese a compliment, while attempting to put the debates and speculation about this appointment to rest. He said he had come to Rochester because, of all the available dioceses he was asked to choose from, Rochester had simply been the best.[4]

Rather than live in the bishop's mansion, Sheen chose to live in an apartment in the same building that housed his offices. This allowed retiring Bishop Kearney to live out his days in what had been his home for nearly three decades. Sheen had no need for a mansion; he just wanted enough space in his home for a chapel, so that he could continue his practice of the Holy Hour.

Sheen spent his first night in his new diocese at St. Bernard's Seminary. This not only proclaimed to the seminarians that their new leader was also their servant but also allowed Sheen to meet them all on the personal level that he found to be so vital. The most important domain of a bishop, Sheen wrote in his autobiography, "is his relationship to brother priests and religious."[5]

Bishop Kearney arranged the beautiful ninety-minute installation ceremony for Sheen, which was held the next day at the cathedral. Over a thousand people attended, including over forty bishops. More than half the invited were laity, as Sheen had requested.

A large reception followed at the Manger Hotel, and then there was a civic welcome at the largest hall in Rochester, the War Memorial. Although the crowd was a massive four thousand people strong, this didn't fill half of the hall. If it disturbed Sheen that he was no longer pulling in full-capacity crowds, he didn't show it. Instead he was celebratory. At one point he pretended to conduct the band in a rousing number of "Hello, Dolly!," and throughout the evening he remained every inch the smiling host.

THE BEGINNING OF A BEAUTIFUL FRIENDSHIP
Later that month Sheen visited the Church of St. Francis de Sales in Geneva. The assistant pastor there, Michael

Hogan, was immediately impressed by Sheen's humility. When he asked the bishop what his intentions were with the diocese, Sheen asked Hogan in all sincerity, what was he interested in seeing happen?

Hogan was struck by the unusual reply. He had expected Sheen to be like other bishops he had known: intent on implementing his own agenda. Instead he found that Sheen was not only open to suggestions but willing to hear and give precedence to the ideas others might have.

Sheen was also impressed by Hogan. He returned to the parish some weeks later to ask him to become his secretary. Upon arriving, Sheen discovered that both Hogan and the pastor of the church were sick. Desiring to be of service, Sheen pitched in with the daily duties. He stepped into the confessional for one of his favorite tasks of the priesthood. Parishioners were shocked to learn later that Sheen had been the one to hear their confessions that day.

Sheen felt that humor and humility went hand and hand, and he saw Father Hogan demonstrate this truth time and again. The priest had a deep respect for Sheen, and he also knew how to exchange quips with him. Sheen enjoyed this immensely and would go on to quote the secretary a number of times in his memoirs. One story Sheen liked to tell regarded his car.

Thanks to a deal Hogan struck with a car dealership in Rochester, Sheen was leased a new automobile every year. He marveled at this generosity, although he felt it was "typical of the kindness"[6] of the people he encountered in Rochester. He told Hogan, "When the Good Lord was on earth, He had to go around Jerusalem on an ass; but it is my privilege... to be driving a Plymouth around the diocese."

Hogan agreed, "Yes, but you still have an ass to drive you."[7]

Sheen loved all of the priests in his diocese. He utilized his phenomenal memory to remember all their names. He would visit them when they were sick.

Sheen had been inspired by the spirit of Vatican II, and he eagerly implemented changes in the administrative structure of his diocese in hopes that they would help to both strengthen the priesthood and empower the laity. He wanted to make sure that the voices of all in his diocese were heard.

He set up an unprecedented "priests' council," a senate made up initially of thirteen priests, two of them hand-picked by Sheen and eleven voted on by the priests of the diocese. "I want men of faith around me," he said.[8] He also wanted the priests in the diocese to have a say in choosing their leaders, believing the voice of Christ could be heard in their decisions.

Sheen created a board of laymen to review candidates for the priesthood within the diocese. He asked that the reviews include psychological testing to help determine seminarians' readiness for the tasks that lay ahead of them. Sheen believed it was only fair that the laity had some say about who their spiritual servants were going to be.[9]

A TIMELY ORDINATION

Father Andrew Apostoli concurs that Bishop Sheen "profoundly loved the priesthood."[10] Now a Franciscan Friar of the Renewal and the vice-postulator for the cause of Bishop Sheen's canonization, Apostoli was a simple

Capuchin brother when Sheen was assigned to the diocese of Rochester. He was doubly excited by the news because, as a fourth-year theology student in the seminary, he would be ordained in the spring. He was both thrilled and humbled at the idea that someone as prominent and holy as Sheen would be presiding over the ceremony.

On the Sunday before Christmas, Sheen was scheduled to make a public appearance in Geneva, New York, home of the Capuchins. The brothers excitedly made plans to see him. Sheen had been making the rounds all over his diocese almost from the moment his plane had touched down. He wanted to meet and greet all the people that he could, and the Capuchins wanted to be counted among that number.

Sadly, Apostoli would have to miss the event. He had recently been ordained a deacon and already had a commitment to preach somewhere else. He was deeply disappointed that just when the bishop would be in town, he was needed out of town, but nothing could be done.

After fulfilling his duty, Apostoli returned to his seminary at around three o'clock in the afternoon. The bishop was scheduled to leave Geneva between noon and one o'clock. But as Apostoli stepped out of his car, a brother rushed out to meet him, shouting, "Hurry! Bishop Sheen will be here in ten minutes!"

Sheen was behind schedule. And when he finally made his public appearance, the bishop had spotted the friars in the crowd. "Do I have Capuchins in my diocese?" he asked. When he found out that he did, he learned where they were staying and told them to expect him later in the day.

When Sheen met Apostoli, the formation director told the bishop that the brother would be up for ordination early in the new year. He asked Sheen, "Will you ordain him?"

"Yes, I will," Sheen replied immediately.

Since the Franciscan Friars were a religious order, they ran on a different schedule than the diocese. Their friars were often ordained earlier in the year than the diocesan clergy. Since Apostoli was the only fourth-year theology student among the friars, he alone would be with Sheen on the altar. This promised to be a very special and intimate experience.

The friars hit a snag soon after Christmas when they tried to schedule the ordination with Sheen's office. The new secretary was still getting his bearings and was overwhelmed by the number of invitations and obligations the bishop had. Everyone wanted Sheen, he told the friars. He offered them two alternatives: the first was to have Apostoli ordained with the diocesan clergy later in the year; the second was to have Apostoli ordained early, as planned, but by Bishop Kearney.

Apostoli chose the second option because he had his "heart set" on an early ordination. But for two days he struggled with his deep disappointment. On the third day his formation director handed him a ray of hope in the form of a letter.

"Mail this," he said. Apostoli looked at the envelope. It was addressed to Bishop Fulton Sheen and had about eight stamps on it. It was marked "Personal" and "Confidential." The friars had to try.

Within two days Fulton Sheen himself called
Apostoli's director. "I told you I would ordain that young
man!" he proclaimed. Sheen was true to his word. Father
Andrew Apostoli was the first priest that Bishop Fulton
Sheen ordained in the diocese of Rochester.[11]

SOUL-SEARCHING

In 1968 Sheen flew back to Peoria, the site of his first parish
assignment, to celebrate mass for the hundredth anniversary
of St. Patrick Church. At the reception at least 250 people
swarmed around Sheen, who was still dressed in his ceremo-
nial vestments, complete with miter and crosier. While
shaking hands and recalling the old days with familiar faces,
the bishop spotted a face in the crowd he didn't know. He
told Father Thomas Henseler, a priest assigned to St.
Patrick's, "Get me that woman.... I see trouble in her eyes."

This amazed Father Henseler. The woman was at least
seventy-five feet away and a stranger to Sheen. But
Henseler knew her and was aware that she was suffering
from serious marital problems. What did the bishop see? It
was as though he had some kind of spiritual radar.

Henseler went and told the woman that the bishop
wished to speak to her. She must have been surprised. She
had not planned to attend the anniversary Mass. In fact,
she had not been to Mass in five years. Her ticket to this
event had been offered to her on the spur of the moment.

Sheen abandoned the crowd and the press and took the
woman into a room for a private meeting. The bishop surely
heard her confession and her woes. Twenty minutes later
the two emerged from the room, and Sheen told Henseler

that the woman would be attending Mass on Sunday from then on. He called her "one of God's children." Then he dove back into the crowd for more socializing.[12]

The bishop seemed able to look into the soul of another woman, a flight attendant he knew in New York. She was taking classes with him one day when they arrived at the subject of confession and sin. She stopped him and refused to go on with the lesson. Sheen asked her to give him one hour to speak on the subject. If by the end of that hour she felt the same way, she could leave.

As the end of the hour neared, the woman reacted fiercely. "Now I'll never join the Church after what I have heard!" she insisted.

Sheen could not understand how his message of mercy was resulting in such a violent refusal. He looked at her and asked, "Have you ever had an abortion?"

The woman became quiet and then admitted that she had. Sheen recognized that it was not the sacrament of penance that was holding the woman back but her own shame. She was behaving like an animal caught in a trap, convinced that the hand that was trying to free her intended to do her more harm. Sheen eventually heard her confession, received her back into the church and baptized her next child.[13]

THE BISHOP IN THE SYNAGOGUE
Sheen often made day trips to the different corners of his diocese, which made tracking him down sometimes difficult. He was welcomed at more than the Catholic churches of his diocese; Protestant and Jewish leaders opened their doors to

him as well. Rabbi Philip Bernstein joked that if the Catholic people of Rochester wanted to see their bishop, they would have to go to a Jewish service to find him.[14]

Soon after his arrival in Rochester, Sheen was invited to deliver an address at a welcoming reception at Temple B'rith Kodesh. He spoke before an audience of over two thousand people. Sheen believed that Jews and Christians shared the vocation from God to be revolutionists. It was because of this that they faced persecution. This shared lot should, he believed, result in unity.

Sheen, always one to practice what he preached, made friends among his Jewish counterparts, often engaging in dialogue and sitting in on events, such as a colloquium on Catholic-Jewish relationships with Rabbi Marc H. Tanenbaum. Rabbi Tanenbaum was younger than Sheen but a prominent religious leader during the same era who was also well-known for his ecumenical efforts. Tanenbaum had the unique distinction of being the only rabbi present at the Second Vatican Council, where he acted as an official observer.[15]

Herbert Bronstein, who served the historic Temple of B'rith Kodesh and is now a well-respected rabbi active in interfaith ministry, compared Sheen to Saint Jerome. This scholarly saint from the Middle Ages had also consulted with the rabbis of his day. Not everyone described the bishop's friendly relations with the Jewish people in glowing terms. Detractors were vocal about their concerns, and bigots even accused him of being heretical.

Sheen did not let these people's opinions—or their threats—influence him. Rather he challenged them: "Few people on the face of the earth suffered as much in recent years as the Jews. Shall Christians despise them who through suffering have become more like our Master than they themselves become through their hate and criticism?"[16]

FROM CROSS TO CRUCIFIX

Even Christians who have accepted Christ and believe in him can use a *metanoia*, or what the church calls "a conversion of the heart." It is not enough to just believe; one must also love. In his work with converts, Sheen came to learn that

> the crisis of conversion is sometimes spiritual rather than moral. This is frequent among those who…lead as Christ-like a life as they know how.…The crisis begins in those souls at the moment when they either recognize that they have tremendous potentialities that have not been exercised or else begin to yearn for a religious life that will make greater demands on them.…The growing sense of dissatisfaction with their own ordinariness is accompanied by a passionate craving for surrender, sacrifice and abandonment to God's Holy Will.…[It is] a shift from mediocrity to love.…The soul hears Christ saying, "Be you therefore perfect, as also your heavenly Father is perfect" (Matt. 5:48).[17]

Perhaps it is surprising that even people who are considered "holy" can have a conversion. Working with the poor and in the missions and there seeing "the poverty of good men and women who were spending themselves and being spent for Christ"[18] impressed upon the bishop a sense of poverty in himself. This was not the kind of poverty for which one should strive; rather it was a feeling of unworthiness. He became more aware of his own sinful nature and weak tendencies. He felt that he was far from where the Lord wanted him to be.

This self-realization inspired him to take action, even in tiny and symbolic ways. He exchanged the cross he usually wore on the end of his chain for a crucifix—and not just any crucifix. It was one that the nuns had sold to the Jewish jeweler in exchange for thirty pieces of silver. The bishop wore it as a private and meaningful representation of the suffering the Lord had endured bodily, with the added reminder of his betrayal.

Bishop Sheen wanted to live in allegiance to Jesus in imitation of Saint Paul, who wrote in his Letter to the Corinthians, "I decided to know nothing among you except Jesus Christ and him crucified" (1 Corinthians 2:2).

Rochester provided Sheen with his Calvary. From the very beginning of his bishopric, he was "humbled,"[19] according to his secretary. Father Hogan traveled around the diocese with the bishop and witnessed firsthand how the triumph of the "entry into Rochester" grew sour with failure and rejection.

A pattern began to emerge. Sheen would be disappointed by the lack of interest his own flock showed in the lectures, retreats and dinners he offered them. In giving a retreat to college students in downtown Rochester, the bishop arrived to find that his audience filled only a single row of seats. After a requiem Mass he hosted a dinner for clergy, and in a generous spirit that resembled that of the king giving the banquet in Matthew 22:1–10, he went out into the street to invite passersby to join the feast, but there were few takers.

When a smattering of people showed up at yet another talk he had scheduled—this time in the largest auditorium in Rochester—the bishop was grieved again. In a private moment he echoed the Lord's sentiments about the prophet who was not accepted in his own country (see Matthew 13:57): "The whole world comes to hear Fulton Sheen, except his own diocese."[20]

In a letter to Clare Boothe Luce, Sheen recognized the suffering he was undergoing as a necessary and holy trial. "The work is very hard," he admitted, "but I love it. I feel that I am sharing in the contemporary crucifixion, and it gives me much joy."[21]

The bishop did not spend his days feeling sorry for himself. He knew that even on the cross Christ continued to serve, preach and heal. Even on Calvary Christ was not alone; others hung on crosses with him. Sheen recognized the others suffering alongside him, and he resolved to help them as best he could.

ROCKING THE BOAT

"Africa was the first [continent] to share the Cross of Christ,"[22] Sheen said, referring to the scriptural record that Simon of Cyrene (in northern Africa) was forced to help Jesus carry the cross (see Matthew 27:32). Sheen saw meaningful symbolism in this, and he took a great interest in the plight of the black people in his diocese.

The majority of those suffering poverty in Rochester were black, and Sheen took it upon himself to work at relieving their double burdens of unemployment and inadequate housing. He didn't believe that a priest was a social worker, however, but rather a spiritual worker. "We lose our souls not only because we do evil things, but because we neglect to do good: the buried talent, the unmarked second mile, the passing by the wounded. How often in the Gospel condemnation follows because 'we did nothing.'"[23]

Like much of the country at that time, Rochester was a diocese divided over race relations. Eastman Kodak was particularly singled out in this civil rights battle as a company that had failed to give enough jobs to black people. In a speech delivered before the Chamber of Commerce, Sheen likened this shameful situation of inner-city poverty and prejudice, in the middle of what should have otherwise been a lovely city, to a beautiful woman with a pimple on her nose. To remove this blemish he suggested an "ointment of humility, love and service."[24]

While bravely spoken, the speech resulted in wounded egos and closed checkbooks. Rochester, it seemed, was more like an attractive teenager than a grown woman, an adolescent who would rather pretend she didn't have a pimple and was then mortified when someone noticed it.

As had happened previously with his ecumenical efforts, the bishop began receiving disapproving and angry letters. Prejudiced people wrote to say that Sheen had spoken out of turn or simply to express their unwillingness to integrate the workplace. He once again ignored them.

Sheen did not intend to upset people or hurt their feelings; he simply wanted to shake them up, as Jesus did once he entered Jerusalem. He preferred to challenge and confront people and problems head-on. He was honest, but he did not accuse. He preferred the gentler tactic of simply holding up a spiritual mirror.

Sometimes people did not like what they saw in their own reflections. One time Sheen held up that mirror in front of Lyndon B. Johnson, the president of the United States. Johnson had called for a "National Day for Peace and Reconciliation," but Sheen saw hypocrisy in this. Originally mum on the subject of war, he had come to see that outside the good of combating Communism, the Vietnam War served no other useful purpose.

During a homily at Sacred Heart Cathedral on July 30, 1967, Sheen made his first public statement regarding Vietnam. President Johnson, he said, should mark his National Day for Peace and Reconciliation by immediately calling back all the American forces he had sent to Vietnam. He should then ask the Lord's forgiveness for the sins of the United States and "go and be reconciled to your northern Vietnam brother."[25]

The pope had already denounced the war, so Sheen's statements were in keeping with the church. Still he created murmurings—particularly among conservatives, who were usually in agreement with Sheen. People were beginning to wonder, was Sheen no longer anti-Communist? Had he defected to the liberal camp?

In a television interview with David Frost two years after his public statements about Vietnam, Sheen did not waver in his opinion. He stated that an offensive war could never be justified as Christian. In fact, the only war Christians truly were called to declare was the war against war itself.

Cardinal Spellman held the opposite view. He believed that the war in Vietnam was necessary to combat evil, and he even compared American soldiers to "holy crusaders."[26]

THROWING STONES

A battle Sheen continued to fight was for affordable inner-city housing. He addressed this problem in a news conference outside Immaculate Conception Church, which was located in one of the areas most in need of assistance. Afterward a black woman holding a baby approached him. Her statement was half challenge, half invitation: "You ought to see where I live."

Sheen and Hogan followed her home, where they met her husband and two other children. Her family lived in destitution, and Sheen responded with his trademark generosity. Soon after his visit he arranged for the woman to meet with a real estate agent and hunt for more suitable living quarters in a safer neighborhood. When a home was chosen, the bishop personally paid for its purchase.[27]

Sheen knew he couldn't do the same for every needy family in Rochester, but there had to be a way to help others who were in a similar situation. Why not, he thought, give a barely used church and its surrounding real estate to the federal government to transform into a hundred or even two hundred units of new, clean, safe and affordable living quarters for low-income families? Sheen found inspiration in the story of Saint Laurence, who gave away church vessels to help the poor.

He sat down and wrote a letter to the Secretary of Housing, the Honorable Robert C. Weaver. He made the offer, explaining:

> We do this not because we do not need [the church and real estate], nor because we are not finding new expressions of apostolate...nor because it is a burden to our budget.... We are under the Gospel-imperative not to be just a receiving Church, but a giving Church,...not just a ministering Church, but a surrendering Church. We are moved by the Spirit to do this in order to crash the giving barrier, just as technology crashed the sound barrier.[28]

It was an idea with noble intention. The offer pleased Mr. Weaver very much. He informed Sheen that the government wished that churches all over the country would donate property for that very purpose. Sheen drew up a list of properties he could offer, with the hope that there would be one that the Department of Housing and Urban Development could truly work with.[29]

The Church of St. Bridget was chosen. It took up one square block of the inner city. With only a hundred parishioners, it seemed a good choice. All the arrangements were made through the proper channels except the one that was the most important: the people of St. Bridget's parish.

The announcement, made on Ash Wednesday of 1968, that "the Diocese of Rochester, its bishop, its clergy and its *people*" (emphasis mine) were offering "Church property to the propertyless"[30] may have been one of sincerity and goodwill, but it came as a surprise to the little parish of St. Bridget. Some people thought the church was the one spot of hope in an otherwise hopeless neighborhood. Why pull it down when other property stood empty and could be used for housing instead?

There was an immediate uproar. Students at the community college took up the cause of the little church, at a time when protests and marches were very much in vogue. College girls armed with placards arranged a demonstration outside Sheen's office, portraying the bishop as someone who stripped parishes from the poor and defenseless. Nasty letters found their way to the bishop's desk.

One evening just four days after the Ash Wednesday announcement, Sheen was on his way to visit a school when he found himself surrounded by several hundred angry people. They hurled pebbles and curses at him as his car passed by. Sheen was so shaken by the blatant hostility that he withdrew his offer to the government that very night.

The bishop was not used to being on the receiving end of venomous condemnation. He was more accustomed to being respected and admired. To see the very people he was trying to help suddenly turn on him was traumatic.

What made matters worse was that it wasn't just the public that was against him. After escaping the angry crowd, Sheen arrived at his office to find a petition on his desk signed by twenty-two priests of the diocese of Rochester. While not written in an angry or judgmental style, the message was clear. The priests expressed their objections over the handling of the matter and strongly urged the bishop to reconsider his decision. Sheen loved his priests dearly, and receiving a statement from so many of them expressing their collective disapproval crushed him.[31]

Commonweal magazine supported Sheen, comparing the bishop's actions to that of a prophet. The magazine article reminded its readers that when authority behaves in a prophetic fashion, it may make people uncomfortable and angry.[32]

Even Father Francis H. Vogt, the pastor of St. Bridget, was forgiving. He admitted to having great admiration for the "tremendous" idea that inspired Sheen's actions. He speculated that had the parish been consulted, Sheen's plan may have even met with success.[33]

As it was, not only was Sheen's idea abandoned, but years later the Church of St. Bridget was as well. It had not been a vibrant parish to begin with, and a great many of the protesters had not been parishioners but rather passersby who wanted to join in the fray. Once the battle was won, the "crusaders" lost their passion for the cause and went home, leaving St. Bridget's unchanged if not worse for the wear. The parish continued to dwindle, and the church eventually closed. Years later, standing alone in a state of disrepair and useful neither as a church nor for housing for the poor, the shell of St. Bridget's would seem to Sheen's eyes a testament to his failure.[34]

However, Sheen was never one to give up completely. He set up a modest, grass-roots program called the Bishop Sheen Housing Foundation (later the Bishop Sheen Ecumenical Housing Foundation).[35] Through it he was able to give the gift of home ownership to eighteen families in Rochester before he retired.

❧ 9 ❧

Retreading, Not Retiring

In May of 1969, less than three years after being assigned to Rochester, Fulton Sheen walked into the study of Pope Paul VI and announced that he would be resigning from his post. Sheen was nearly seventy-five years old, the age when he was required to submit his retirement.

The pope made no indication that he had even heard Sheen and brought up a completely different topic for discussion. After indulging the pontiff for ten minutes, Fulton asked the pope again if it would be the pleasure of his holiness to accept his resignation as bishop of Rochester. Pope Paul VI started another conversation on an entirely separate church matter. Only when Sheen asked a third time did the pope accept the resignation. By October of that year it was official.

The pope allowed Sheen to pick his successor, and Sheen did not hesitate. He had had a gut feeling about Monsignor Joseph Hogan's suitability almost from the moment he met him. The monsignor was the brother of his personal secretary and friend, Father Michael Hogan. The Hogan brothers had both proven themselves to be good and trustworthy priests. The torch was passed, and Sheen moved back to his beloved city of Manhattan.

Sheen said that although he resigned, he did not retire. He simply "took on another kind of work."[1] At that time he had about a decade yet to live, and he spent his last days in typical Sheen style, with tireless service to the church in ways best suited to his talents.

He continued preaching, speaking on the lecture circuit, teaching catechism and apologetics, entering into dialogue with nonbelievers and leading retreats for priests. Before he died Sheen had accumulated the wealth of sixty years of experience in the priesthood, making him a veritable walking treasure box of wisdom, which he freely opened to the younger generation.

The best nugget of advice Sheen felt he could give young priests was the resolution "to make a continuous hour of meditation in the presence of the Blessed Sacrament every day."[2] Sheen believed it was an easy resolution to remember making and one that, if truly and humbly practiced, would set the tone for a successful priesthood.

Sheen was given the honor of two new titles after his resignation: assistant at the pontifical throne and titular archbishop of Newport in Wales. In addition the Vatican appointed him to the Commission for Non-Believers.[3]

The first honor didn't excite Sheen very much. It simply affirmed what he already knew about himself and had striven to be all through his career as a priest: a loyal page at the throne of Peter. The second title gave him the right to be addressed as "*Arch*bishop Fulton J. Sheen." As a title only, however, it left Sheen free from the worry of having to take over the responsibilities of an entire archdiocese—and of having to move to Wales!

Back in New York Sheen was as far removed from thrones as he had ever been in his life. Although he was seventy-five, he decided against having a housekeeper for his three-room apartment. He made his own bed and did his own dishes. He admitted to putting off the dusting, however, joking that the dust served as a humble reminder that he had come from dust and would one day return to dust.

Near Death

And to dust he almost did return in July 1977. Shortly after a trip to Lourdes, Fulton Sheen underwent open heart surgery.

Heart disease ran in Sheen's family. His father, Newt, had died of a heart attack in 1944, as did his closest brother, Joe, in 1955. His father and other brother, Tom, suffered from Alzheimer's, which thankfully Fulton did not inherit. Fulton had officiated at the funerals of his father and brothers, as well as of his mother in 1943, when she died of cancer.[4] His brother Al passed away while Fulton was ill himself and unable to travel.[5]

Before entering the hospital Sheen had not appeared ill. He had slowed down some, but that was easily attributed to age. A checkup showed that liquid was filling his lungs, and Sheen became an official cardiac emergency.

Now eighty-two, Sheen was the oldest person to undergo open heart surgery at the hospital.[6] As he lay near death on the operating table, the surgeons worked quickly. They repaired the damage, implanted a pacemaker and pumped seventy pints of donated blood into his body. While still recovering in the intensive care unit, a priest came and celebrated Mass at the foot of his bed. Always carrying a deep love for the Eucharist, Sheen sat up and concelebrated the Mass as best he could, which amazed his doctor.[7]

A month later Sheen required surgery again, this time for his prostate. He was deluged with get-well cards, was visited by such well-known holy figures as Mother Teresa and New York's Cardinal Terence Cooke and received phone calls from President Jimmy Carter and Pope Paul VI.[8]

This hospital stay was much longer. Sheen required a four-month recovery period and was bedridden for most of it. Early on he was in a lot of pain. At one point he was sure he was dying.

He lay in intensive care, moaning and writhing in pain. A nurse interpreted his physical agony as emotional or mental distress. A priest psychiatrist came in with the goal of lifting him out of his supposed depression. Being "asked Freudian questions as [he] was dying"[9] angered Sheen because of its uselessness and its lack of spirituality. The experience was not unlike the Lord's on the cross, when to slake his thirst he was offered vinegar on a sponge.

Between the dual tortures of the empty words of the droning psychiatrist and of fresh pains in his own body, Sheen heard the nurse say that the patient nearby was dying.

At that moment Sheen had an insight into the value of his pain, and he immediately offered up his sufferings for the salvation of his neighbor's soul. Unable to raise his hand, Sheen lifted a single finger, made a tiny sign of the cross and gave him absolution. At that moment the man died.

From the cross Jesus won the forgiveness of sins for the world. As an ordained priest commissioned by Christ, Sheen was able to transfer the Lord's forgiveness to the man in the next bed, despite his own excruciating pain.

A few months later the man's widow visited Sheen and told him, "I saw [what you did]." She thanked him, saying the archbishop's actions for her husband that night had been a source of consolation for her. She gave Sheen a Jewish long-life medal to show her appreciation.[10]

CHICKEN SOUP FOR THE BISHOP'S SOUL

When Sheen was finally able to leave the hospital, his already slender frame, which was estimated to weigh no more than 125 pounds at its heaviest, had become frighteningly thin. His doctor, Michael Bruno, noticed the concerned looks on the faces of the journalists who had gathered at the hospital to report on Sheen's discharge. He told them that while the bishop's appetite was poor, once he began eating properly again, his looks should improve.

Sheen, however, had never been much of an eater. While he claimed in his autobiography that he found fasting difficult,[11] gluttony was far from being a weakness with him. He had a preference for sweets (that tea and candy at the headquarters of the Society of the Propagation of the Faith was as much for him as for the women) and favored chocolate above all.

Back in the seminary he had suffered from ulcers, which ultimately required surgery to have part of an intestine removed. For years he had digestive problems and stomach pains. He was often seen shifting food around his plate at social events.[12]

Chicken, with its mild properties, would have been a wise staple in his diet, but Sheen detested chicken. Whenever he was expected to dine at an event, his secretaries were sure to inform his hosts ahead of time that the bishop was not to be served chicken of any kind. This aversion could be traced to his days back at the farm, where part of his job had been to assist with the slaughter of the chickens. Sheen estimated that he had wrung the necks of over twenty thousand of them during his childhood. He joked that as a result of this, he suffered from "night-hens" rather than nightmares.[13]

After his hospital stay the archbishop became increasingly frail. Once, while Sheen prepared to record the narration for a biblical film, Rabbi Tanenbaum, who had secured the project for Sheen, noticed how gaunt his friend had become and how difficult it was for the archbishop to digest food. The film's producer, John Heyman, presented Sheen with a bowl of chicken soup. The archbishop accepted it gratefully and even pronounced it a lifesaver. So chicken turned out to be the one food that was able to sustain Sheen when he was unable to eat anything else.[14]

In January of 1979 Sheen was invited to be the main speaker at the National Prayer Breakfast in Washington, D.C. His doctor thought the trip was unwise, but since the archbishop was determined to make it, he accompanied

Sheen as a precaution. The Reverend Billy Graham was asked to prepare a sermon as a backup, just in case Sheen found himself unable to perform his duty.

Everyone in the ballroom watched the priest make his way feebly to the podium and then turn to face President Jimmy Carter. "Mr. President," he began, "you are a sinner." He continued, "I am a sinner. We are all sinners." Sheen's subsequent sermon on everyone's need for God proved to be an unforgettable experience for all who heard him.[15]

POPE JOHN PAUL THE GREAT

"I believe that Pope John Paul II will go down in history as one of the great Pontiffs of all times," Fulton Sheen wrote in his autobiography.[16] This is truly an impressive prophecy, given the fact that John Paul II was pope for barely a year before Sheen passed away. He would become the third longest serving pope in the history of the Catholic church and would prove to be, just as Sheen had foreseen, an uncommon man of many gifts. He would leave this earth with many proclaiming him "great" and a "saint."

Sheen recognized the Polish poet and philosopher for the mystic that he was. In describing the pontiff, Sheen was able to summarize succinctly the manner in which John Paul II would live out his term as pope:

> He preaches…the freedom to do whatever you *ought*, and oughtness implies a goal, a purpose in living and meaning. His *mystique* affirms the sacredness of life, the right to worship God according to the light of con-science, and the commitment to human rights, which is very like that which is written in our own Declaration of

Independence: that all of our rights and liberties come
to us from our Creator.[17]

On reaching his sixtieth anniversary in the priesthood,
Sheen received a letter of congratulations from John Paul
II. His holiness referred to the archbishop as his "Beloved
Brother in Christ" for whom he felt "fraternal affection."
He praised Sheen's lifelong zeal in serving the church and
commended him "to the intercession of the Blessed Virgin
Mary, Mother of God and Mother of priests."[18]

Sheen wrote back to tell the pope that he prayed for
him as "for another Gregory the Great." He felt that the
poet Slowacki was prophesying about John Paul when he
wrote, "A Slav Pope will sweep out the Churches and make
them clean within." Sheen added his own wistful desire to
be young again, if only to see what light the Lord would
bring to the world through the new Vicar of Christ.[19]

One reason for Sheen's adulation of the young pope
must certainly have been a reaction to the pontiff's nine-
day trip to his homeland in June of 1979. Warned by all that
it couldn't be done, as the country was still under
Communist oppression, the pope said Mass in the middle
of Warsaw's Victory Square. The square would turn out to
be well named.

It was assumed that the people of Poland would be too
fearful to come out and greet their countryman, let alone
worship at Mass with him. Nothing could have been further from the truth. Three hundred thousand people
attended the Mass, and three million Poles in all would
flock to see the pope as he made his way across that small

country. As the pope preached to the crowds, the people spontaneously broke into the chant "We want God! We want God!"[20]

In a few short years Communism would collapse and die peacefully in Eastern Europe. A few years later, after Pope John Paul II heeded the call of Our Lady of Fatima and consecrated the world—and especially Russia—to the Immaculate Heart of Mary, the Soviet Union also collapsed. Almost overnight, it seemed, the Communist threat was gone, and Holy Mother Russia was reborn.

SAINT FULTON SHEEN?

On December 9, 1979, Fulton Sheen stood at the impressive podium of St. Patrick Cathedral, practicing the homily he would give at the midnight Mass on Christmas Eve. That evening he died in his apartment. There are conflicting stories as to where his body was found. Some say he was in his chapel; Father Apostoli believes that he died on his way to the chapel. What is known for certain is that Sheen truly believed in and practiced his Holy Hour until the end. He was eighty-four.

Fulton Sheen once wrote, "Death is meant to be our true birth, our beginning. Christianity, in contrast to paganism, always blesses her children's spiritual birth into eternity. In the liturgy, the day on which a saint dies is called his *natilita,* or birthday. The world celebrates a birthday on the day a person is born to physical life; the Church celebrates it when a person is born to eternal life."[21]

Sheen's death fell on the day *after* a Marian feast day, the Feast of the Immaculate Conception. While not exactly what the bishop had hoped for, it is interesting to note that December 9 is the Feast of Saint Juan Diego, the simple peasant man who saw the Virgin Mother appear as Our Lady of Guadalupe. Father Apostoli has speculated that if Sheen is ever made a saint, his feast day could be observed on December 10.

Tributes from around the world were heard on radio and published in newspapers. For two days his body lay in state at St. Patrick Cathedral, and thousands of mourners filed by—many reaching out to touch his hands. His funeral took place on December 13, and Archbishop Edward O'Meara, friend and successor of Sheen as the national director of the Society of the Propagation of the Faith, officiated.

"The vocation of Fulton Sheen is consummated," O'Meara proclaimed in his eulogy. "He has responded with one final 'yes' to the call of God."[22]

Although Sheen asked in his will to be buried in Calvary Cemetery, Cardinal Cooke decided to have his body interred in a crypt beneath the altar of St. Patrick's. It was an honor usually reserved for archbishops of New York and rectors of the cathedral, but for fifty years Sheen had preached from that altar, and some of his sermons were the best ever proclaimed there. It was a fitting final resting place.

In 2002 the cause for the canonization of Fulton Sheen was opened, and a new title has been added to his roster: "Servant of God." Is Fulton Sheen a saint?

Let us recall his traits and gifts: consummate priest; lover of Christ—especially in the Eucharist; gifted preacher; devotee of Mary; lover of people; helper of the poor; compassionate confessor; talented teacher; convert-maker; dedicated missionary; dogged fundraiser; media star. "If he ever becomes a saint," Father Apostoli told this author, "he will be the only one who has ever won an Emmy."

We must not forget that Sheen was a man of great vitality, humor and humanity. In the years before the rage of "reality television," it was his goal to bring the reality of God into homes and hearts all over the world. He did this with plainspoken truth, in easy-to-understand spirituality, without judgment or condescension and with the right dash of wit. Greg Hildebrandt has said, "I would hate to see Sheen become a plaster statue. He was holy—not holier-than-thou. To be saintly is to be incredibly human, which makes Fulton Sheen a saint already in my book."[23]

"I HAVE HEARD MY MOTHER SPEAK OF YOU"
Fulton J. Sheen once wrote, "How God will judge, I know not, but I trust that He will see me with mercy and compassion. I am only certain that there will be three surprises in Heaven. First of all, I will see some people there whom I never expected to see. Second, there will be a number whom I expect to be there who will not be there. And, even relying on His mercy, the biggest surprise of all may be that I will be there."[24]

Archbishop O'Meara, Sheen's longtime friend, did not think it would be surprising to find that Sheen had made it to heaven. He had these departing words for Sheen's soul: "We trust you to the care of your 'Lovely Lady dressed in blue.' We pray that Jesus has already said: 'I've heard my Mother speak of you.'"[25]

It is the hope of this author that his welcome into heaven was like the reception he received from Pope John Paul II just two months before he died. It was October 2, 1979. The young Polish pope, who would become famous for his travels around the world, was making his first trip to the United States. One of the first stops on his journey was St. Patrick Cathedral in New York City.

A huge crowd had assembled both inside and outside St. Patrick's. Pope John Paul II entered the cathedral to an enthusiastic response. With Cardinal Terence Cooke by his side, the pope made his way up the long aisle to the sanctuary. Once there he looked around, searching for one face in particular. Finally he asked, "Where is Archbishop Sheen?"

Apparently the pontiff had expected to see the archbishop seated in a place of prominence. The pope had seen episodes of *Life Is Worth Living* in his younger days, even crediting the program for helping him to learn English.[26] Like Sheen, he had the habit of writing the initials "J.M.J." on the top of paperwork and correspondence.[27]

Cardinal Cooke sent his secretary to hunt for the fragile archbishop. Sheen was found in the back of the church, behind the altar, in the small but beautiful "Lady's Chapel," where the Blessed Sacrament was kept.

When Sheen attempted to kneel before the pope and kiss his ring, John Paul II held him up and pulled him into an embrace. Those in the cathedral broke out into a thunderous applause, which grew into a seven-minute standing ovation. As the pope held the frail bishop in his arms, he told Sheen, "You have written and spoken well of the Lord Jesus. You are a loyal son of the Church."[28]

Notes

CHAPTER ONE: A PROPHECY FOR A PROPHET

1. Fulton J. Sheen, *Treasure in Clay: The Autobiography of Fulton J. Sheen* (San Francisco: Ignatius, 1993), p. 12. This autobiography was the primary source of information for this book.

2. Sheen, *Treasure in Clay*, p. 12.

3. Sheen, *Treasure in Clay*, p. 12.

4. Sheen, *Treasure in Clay*, p. 29.

5. Sheen, *Treasure in Clay*, p. 30.

6. Sheen, *Treasure in Clay*, p. 18.

7. Sheen, *Treasure in Clay*, p. 8.

8. Thomas C. Reeves, *America's Bishop: The Life and Times of Fulton J. Sheen* (San Francisco: Encounter, 2001), p. 11.

9. Sheen, *Treasure in Clay*, pp. 16, 30.

10. Sheen, *Treasure in Clay*, p. 17.

11. Sheen, *Treasure in Clay*, p. 323.

12. Sheen, *Treasure in Clay*, p. 10.

13. Sheen, *Treasure in Clay*, p. 10.
14. Sheen, *Treasure in Clay*, p. 6.
15. Fulton J. Sheen, *Lift Up Your Heart: A Guide to Spiritual Peace* (Liguori, Mo.: Liguori, 1998), p. 127.
16. Sheen, *Treasure in Clay*, p. 30.
17. Sheen, *Treasure in Clay*, p. 30.
18. Sheen, *Treasure in Clay*, p. 30.
19. Sheen, *Treasure in Clay*, p. 31.
20. Sheen, *Treasure in Clay*, pp. 31–32.
21. Sheen, *Treasure in Clay*, p. 23.
22. Sheen, *Treasure in Clay*, pp. 28, 41.
23. Sheen, *Treasure in Clay*, p. 41.
24. Reeves, p. 58; Sheen, *Treasure in Clay*, pp. 267–268.
25. Sheen, *Treasure in Clay*, p. 42.
26. Sheen, *Treasure in Clay*, p. 54.
27. Sheen, *Treasure in Clay*, pp. 54–55.
28. Reeves, p. 75.
29. Sheen, *Treasure in Clay*, p. 63.

CHAPTER TWO: A PRIEST FOREVER
1. Sheen, *Treasure in Clay*, p. 64.
2. Bob Harrison, "Metro New York AM Call Letter History," www.oldradio.com.
3. Reeves, p. 110.
4. Reeves, p. 108.
5. Sheen, *Treasure in Clay*, p. 359.
6. Sheen, *Treasure in Clay*, p. 69; Reeves, p. 85.
7. Sheen, *Treasure in Clay*, pp. 335, 337.
8. Sheen, *Treasure in Clay*, p. 254.
9. Reeves, p. 135.

10. Sheen, *Treasure in Clay*, p. 36.
11. Sheen, *Treasure in Clay*, p. 38.
12. Sheen, *Treasure in Clay*, p. 36.
13. Sheen, *Treasure in Clay*, p. 32.
14. Sheen, *Treasure in Clay*, p. 39.
15. Sheen, *Treasure in Clay*, pp. 32–34.
16. Sheen, *Treasure in Clay*, p. 192.
17. Sheen, *Treasure in Clay*, p. 230.
18. George Marlin, Richard P. Rabatin and John L. Swan, eds., *The Quotable Fulton Sheen* (New York: Doubleday, 1989), p. 333.
19. Andrew Apostoli, *Archbishop Fulton J. Sheen, A Prophet for Our Times* (New York: Center for Spiritual Development, 2004), tape 3.
20. Sheen, *Treasure in Clay*, p. 236.
21. Sheen, *Treasure in Clay*, p. 34.
22. Sheen, *Treasure in Clay*, pp. 191–192.
23. Sheen, *Treasure in Clay*, p. 192.
24. Sheen, *Treasure in Clay*, p. 199.
25. Sheen, *Treasure in Clay*, p. 188.
26. Sheen, *Treasure in Clay*, p. 192.
27. Fulton J. Sheen and Patricia Kossman, *From the Angel's Blackboard: The Best of Fulton Sheen* (Liguori, Mo.: Liguori, 1996), p. 188.
28. Fulton J. Sheen, *Peace of Soul* (Liguori, Mo.: Liguori, 1996), p. 202.
29. Reeves, p. 36.
30. Sheen and Kossman, p. 188.
31. Sheen, *Treasure in Clay*, p. 189.
32. Sheen, *Treasure in Clay*, p. 189.

33. Reeves, p. 120.

34. Reeves, p. 304.

35. Reeves, p. 237.

36. Reeves, pp. 236–237.

37. Reeves, pp. 112–113.

38. Reeves, p. 266.

39. Reeves, p. 63.

40. Reeves, p. 63.

41. Reeves, pp. 46–47.

42. Fulton J. Sheen, *Renewal and Reconciliation*, tape 9, conference 18, "The Blessed Mother."

CHAPTER THREE: THE BLESSED MOTHER

1. Marlin, Rabatin and Swan, p. 190.

2. Sheen, *Treasure in Clay*, p. 315.

3. Sheen, *Renewal and Reconciliation,* tape 9.

4. Sheen, *Treasure in Clay*, p. 316.

5. Sheen, *Treasure in Clay*, p. 218.

6. Sheen, *Treasure in Clay*, p. 59.

7. Sheen, *Treasure in Clay*, p. 317.

8. Sheen, *Renewal and Reconciliation*, tape 4, "Celibacy."

9. Sheen, *Treasure in Clay*, p. 204.

10. Sheen, *Treasure in Clay*, pp. 204–206.

11. Sheen, *Treasure in Clay*, p. 206.

12. Sheen, *Treasure in Clay*, p. 92.

13. Sheen, *Treasure in Clay*, pp. 322–323.

14. Sheen, *Treasure in Clay*, p. 323.

15. Sheen, *Treasure in Clay*, p. 317.

16. Sheen, *Treasure in Clay*, pp. 317–318.

17. Sheen, *Treasure in Clay*, p. 318, Reeves, p. 57.

18. Sheen, *Treasure in Clay*, p. 318.
19. Sheen, *Treasure in Clay*, p. 326.
20. Reeves, p. 65
21. Fr. J. Linus Ryan, O. CARM., "Servant of God, Archbishop Fulton J. Sheen," www.carmelites.info.

CHAPTER FOUR: A PIONEER

1. Sheen, *Treasure in Clay*, p. 63.
2. Sheen, *Treasure in Clay*, p. 73.
3. Reeves, p. 230; www.lucyfan.com.
4. Sheen, *Treasure in Clay*, p. 297.
5. Sheen, *Treasure in Clay*, p. 58.
6. Marlin, Rabatin and Swan, p. 52.
7. Marlin, Rabatin and Swan, p. 204.
8. Reeves, p. 230.
9. All quotes and references from Greg Hildebrandt are from telephone interviews with Janel Rodriguez in July and August of 2005.
10. Sheen, *Treasure in Clay*, p. 300.
11. www.imdb.com
12. Sheen, *Treasure in Clay*, p. 110.
13. Apostoli, tape 2, side 2.
14. Sheen, *Treasure in Clay*, p. 134.
15. Sheen, *Treasure in Clay*, p. 133.
16. Sheen, *Treasure in Clay*, pp. 135–136.
17. Reeves, p. 189.
18. Reeves, p. 196.
19. Reeves, p. 192.
20. Sheen, *Treasure in Clay*, pp. 106–107.
21. Sheen, *Treasure in Clay*, pp. 110–111.

22. Telephone interview with Hildebrandt.

23. Apostoli, tape 3, side 2.

24. Reeves, p. 286.

25. Sheen, *Treasure in Clay*, p. 132.

26. Sheen, *Treasure in Clay*, p. 139.

27. Sheen, *Treasure in Clay*, p. 137.

CHAPTER FIVE: "THE BOSS"

1. Reeves, p. 215.

2. Sheen, *Treasure in Clay*, pp. 306–307.

3. Interview with Hildebrandt.

4. Reeves, p. 109.

5. Reeves, p. 109.

6. Kathleen L. Riley, PH.D., *Fulton J. Sheen: An American Response to the Twentieth Century* (Staten Island, N.Y.: Alba, 2004), p. 254.

7. Reeves, p. 215.

8. Sheen, *Treasure in Clay*, p. 100.

9. Sheen, *Treasure in Clay*, p. 74.

10. Interview with Hildebrandt.

11. Riley, p. 242.

12. Fulton J. Sheen, *Renewal and Reconciliation*, tape 13, "Fools for Christ's Sake."

13. Interview with Hildebrandt.

14. Interview with Hildebrandt.

15. Reeves, p. 136.

16. Interview with Hildebrandt.

17. Interview with Hildebrandt.

18. Interview with Hildebrandt.

19. Interview with Hildebrandt.

20. Sheen, *Treasure in Clay,* p. 284.
21. Sheen, *Renewal and Reconciliation,* tape 9, conference 18, "The Blessed Mother."
22. Reeves, p. 214.
23. Sheen, *Treasure in Clay,* p. 118.
24. Sheen, *Treasure in Clay,* p. 89.
25. Sheen, *Treasure in Clay,* pp. 89–90.
26. Sheen, *Treasure in Clay,* pp. 81–82.
27. Sheen, *Treasure in Clay,* p. 82.
28. Sheen, *Treasure in Clay,* p. 87.
29. Reeves, p. 171.
30. Reeves, p. 171.

CHAPTER SIX: A SHEPHERD LOOKS FOR SHEEP

1. Sheen, *Treasure in Clay,* p. 148.
2. Sheen, *Treasure in Clay,* p. 148.
3. Sheen, *Treasure in Clay,* p. 253.
4. Sheen, *Treasure in Clay,* p. 264.
5. Sheen, *Treasure in Clay,* p. 264; Reeves, p. 176; see "Women in History: Clare Booth Luce Biography," Lakewood Public Library, http://www.lkwdpl.org/wihohio/luce-cla.htm.
6. Sheen, *Peace of Soul,* p. 201.
7. Sheen, *Peace of Soul,* p. 224.
8. Sheen, *Peace of Soul,* pp. 225–226.
9. Sheen, *Treasure in Clay,* p. 121.
10. Sheen, *Treasure in Clay,* p. 268.
11. Sheen, *Treasure in Clay,* p. 224.
12. Sheen, *Treasure in Clay,* p. 226.
13. Sheen, *Treasure in Clay,* p. 146.

14. Marlin, Rabatin and Swan, p. 8.

15. Marlin, Rabatin and Swan, p. 9.

16. Sheen, *Treasure in Clay*, pp. 275–276.

17. Sheen, *Treasure in Clay*, pp. 346–347.

18. Marlin, Rabatin and Swan, p. 149.

19. Sheen, *Treasure in Clay*, pp. 146–147.

20. Sheen, *Lift Up Your Heart*, p. 242.

21. Sheen, *Lift Up Your Heart*, p. 243.

22. Riley, p. 248.

23. Riley, p. 249.

24. Sheen, *Treasure in Clay*, p. 253.

25. Sheen, *Treasure in Clay*, pp. 166–167.

CHAPTER SEVEN: BROTHERS IN THE LORD
1. Reeves, pp. 253–254.

2. Sheen, *Treasure in Clay*, p. 314.

3. Sheen, *Peace of Soul*, p. 219.

4. Reeves, p. 314.

5. Sheen, *Treasure in Clay*, p. 72.

6. Sheen, *Treasure in Clay*, p. 230.

7. Sheen, *Treasure in Clay*, p. 102.

8. Sheen, *Treasure in Clay*, p. 5.

9. Sheen, *Treasure in Clay*, pp. 230–231.

10. www.salvationisfromthejews.com

11. Reeves, p. 219.

12. Sheen, *Treasure in Clay*, p. 232.

13. Reeves, p. 267.

14. http://www.brainyquote.com

15. Sheen, *Treasure in Clay*, p. 236.

16. Reeves, p. 263.

17. Riley, p. 258.
18. Sheen, *Treasure in Clay*, p. 281.
19. Reeves, p. 270.
20. Reeves, p. 269.
21. Sheen, *Treasure in Clay*, p. 282.
22. Sheen, *Treasure in Clay*, pp. 286–287.
23. Sheen, *Treasure in Clay*, p. 287.
24. Reeves, p. 261.
25. Sheen, *Treasure in Clay*, p. 285.
26. Reeves, p. 277.
27. Riley, p. 263.
28. Sheen, *Treasure in Clay*, p. 284.
29. Reeves, p. 270.
30. Sheen, *Treasure in Clay*, p. 289.
31. Reeves, p. 261.
32. Sheen, *Treasure in Clay*, p. 248.

CHAPTER EIGHT: BANISHED?

1. Apostoli, tape 1, side 2.
2. Reeves, p. 295.
3. Reeves, p. 296.
4. Reeves, p. 296.
5. Sheen, *Treasure in Clay*, p. 176.
6. Sheen, *Treasure in Clay*, p. 176.
7. Sheen, *Treasure in Clay*, pp. 176–177.
8. Reeves, pp. 303, 315.
9. Riley, p. 282.
10. Apostoli, tape 1, side 2.
11. Apostoli, tape 1, side 2.
12. Reeves, pp. 316–317.

13. Sheen, *Treasure in Clay*, p. 279.

14. Riley, p. 284, footnote 54.

15. Riley, p. 284.

16. Marlin, Rabatin and Swan, p. 148.

17. Sheen, *Peace of Soul*, pp. 230–231.

18. Sheen, *Treasure in Clay*, p. 96.

19. Reeves, p. 300.

20. Reeves, p. 300.

21. Reeves, p. 314.

22. Reeves, p. 302.

23. Marlin, Rabatin and Sway, p. 63.

24. Riley, p. 278.

25. Riley, p. 286; Reeves, p. 309.

26. Reeves, p. 309.

27. Reeves, p. 311.

28. Sheen, *Treasure in Clay*, p. 179.

29. Riley, p. 294.

30. Riley, p. 295.

31. Riley, p. 297.

32. Riley, p. 299.

33. Riley, pp. 300–301.

34. Sheen, *Treasure in Clay*, p. 180.

35. Reeves, p. 321.

CHAPTER NINE: RETREADING, NOT RETIRING

1. Sheen, *Treasure in Clay*, p. 183.

2. Sheen, *Treasure in Clay*, p. 222.

3. Riley, p. 304.

4. Reeves, pp. 149, 349.

5. Reeves, p. 352.

6. Reeves, p. 350.

7. Reeves, p. 350.

8. Reeves, p. 350.

9. Sheen, *Treasure in Clay*, p. 346.

10. Reeves, p. 350; Sheen, *Treasure in Clay*, p. 346.

11. Sheen, *Treasure in Clay*, p. 194.

12. Reeves, p. 35.

13. Sheen, *Treasure in Clay*, p. 172; Reeves, p. 21.

14. Reeves, p. 355.

15. Reeves, p. 353.

16. Sheen, *Treasure in Clay*, p. 244.

17. Sheen, *Treasure in Clay*, p. 245.

18. Sheen, *Treasure in Clay*, p. 242.

19. Sheen, *Treasure in Clay*, p. 243.

20. Charles Sennott and Brian Whitmore, "A Fuse Lit in Poland Helps End Soviet Rule," *The Boston Globe*, April 3, 2005.

21. Sheen, *Peace of Soul*, pp. 219–220.

22. Sheen, *Treasure in Clay*, p. 351. The epilogue is O'Meara's eulogy.

23. Interview with Hildebrandt.

24. Sheen, *Treasure in Clay*, p. 6.

25. Sheen, *Treasure in Clay*, p. 355.

26. Apostoli, tape 1, side 2.

27. Reeves, p. 14; Apostoli, tape 1, side 2.

28. Apostoli, tape 1, side 2; Sheen, *Treasure in Clay*, p. 356; Reeves, p. 357.

Bibliography

Marlin, George, Richard P. Rabatin, John L. Swan, eds. *The Quotable Fulton Sheen*. New York: Doubleday, 1989.

Reeves, Thomas C. *America's Bishop: The Life and Times of Fulton J. Sheen*. San Francisco: Encounter, 2001.

Riley, Kathleen L. *Fulton J. Sheen: An American Response to the Twentieth Century*. Staten Island, N.Y.: Alba, 2004.

Sheen, Fulton J. *Lift Up Your Heart: A Guide to Spiritual Peace*. Liguori, Mo.: Liguori, 1998.

———. *Peace of Soul*. Liguori, Mo.: Liguori, 1996.

———. *Treasure in Clay: The Autobiography of Fulton J. Sheen*. San Francisco: Ignatius, 1993.

Sheen, Fulton J. and Patricia Kossmann. *From the Angel's Blackboard: The Best of Fulton Sheen*. Liguori, Mo.: Liguori, 1996.

AUDIOTAPES:

Apostoli, Andrew. *Archbishop Fulton J. Sheen: A Prophet for Our Times*. Set of three audiotapes. New York: Mustard Seed, 2004.

Sheen, Fulton J. *Renewal and Reconciliation*. A series of tapes of retreats for priests. New York: Minstr-O-Media, 1974.

WEB SITES:

www.brothershildebrandt.com. This is the authorized website of film illustrators Greg and Tim Hildebrandt.

www.salvationisfromthejews.com. This website based on the book *Salvation Is from the Jews: The Role of Judaism in Salvation History* by Roy Schoeman (San Francisco: Ignatius, 2004) offers an in-depth study of the role of Jews and Judaism in God's plan for salvation from Abraham to the Second Coming.

www.imdb.com. Internet Movie Database gives information on Fulton Sheen's television program, *Life Is Worth Living* and his guest appearance on *What's My Line?*